THE WEST BANK WALL

The West Bank Wall

Unmaking Palestine

Ray Dolphin

Introduction by Graham Usher

Pluto Press
London • Ann Arbor, MI

First published 2006 by Pluto Press
345 Archway Road, London N6 5AA
and 839 Greene Street, Ann Arbor, MI 48106

www.plutobooks.com

British Library Cataloguing in Publication Data
A catalogue record for this book is available from the British Library

ISBN 0 7453 2434 7 hardback
ISBN 07453 2433 9 paperback

Library of Congress Cataloging in Publication Data applied for

10 9 8 7 6 5 4 3 2 1

Designed and produced for Pluto Press by
Curran Publishing Services, Norwich

Printed and bound in the European Union by
Antony Rowe Ltd, Chippenham and Eastbourne, England

This book is dedicated to all those affected by the wall. May they hold on to their land and livelihoods.

Contents

Acknowledgements

Research for this book would not have been possible without the many individuals who gave me their valuable time and assistance throughout 2002–5. In particular, I would like to thank Abdul-Latif Khaled and Shareef Omar (Abu Azzam), in Jayous, Mohammed Shaheen in Ras Atiya and Yousef Dirawi in Nu'man. Thanks are also due to the staff of all the municipalities and village councils I visited, in particular Marouf Zahran and Nidal Jaloud in Qalqilya, Taisir Harashi in Qaffin, and Jamal Husseini in Zeita. For their suggestions and encouragement from the start I would also like to thank Jamal Juma and Robyn Long of PENGON.

The book would not have been possible without the support of UNRWA, although the views expressed are the author's and should not be taken to reflect the official views of the United Nations, or UNRWA. I would like to thank especially the UNRWA West Bank Operations Department, in particular Jihad Fararjeh and Adeeb Salman.

I also thank Graham Usher for giving me the idea for the book and for the Introduction. For their suggestions, feedback and comments on the text I am indebted to Lucy Mair, Beverly Milton-Edwards, Susan Rockwell, Janet Symes, Isabel de la Cruz and Stefan Ziegler. Special thanks to Beatrice Metaireau and Majed Abu Kubi, and to UNOCHA for permission to reproduce the maps.

Finally for permission to include longer extracts, I am indebted to Uri Avnery and Gush Shalom, *Ha'aretz* newspaper, and the World Council of Churches.

Preface

Two years ago, when the fence was built here, we had a hard time convincing people in Israel that the purpose of the fence was not security or prevention of suicide bombings, but that there were political and settlement interests. First they separated the people of Jayous from their lands, preventing them from working on it. And now everything is clearly visible: they are passing over the lands to settler possession.

> (Israeli peace campaigner, Uri Avnery, addressing Palestinian and Israeli activists who had come to the West Bank village of Jayous to replant olive trees uprooted behind the wall for the expansion of Zufin settlement.)[1]

In the second part of 2002, Israel began construction of a 'security fence' in the northern West Bank. The project went little noticed initially. The first half of 2002 had witnessed an unprecedented wave of suicide bombings inside Israel and a military offensive by the Israeli Defence Forces that caused widespread destruction to Jenin and other West Bank Palestinian cities. If Israel decided to build an obstacle to protect its citizens from Palestinian assailants – which would have the added benefit of separating the two warring sides – this seemed reasonable – even desirable – in the eyes of many.

However, as construction proceeded of what was alleged to be a temporary, preventative obstacle, disquiet grew. Despite official assurances that the barrier 'does not annex any lands to Israel nor does it establish any borders', large areas of prime Palestinian land were alienated from their owners, whose access became dependent on a gate and permit regime.[2] As for the disclaimer concerning borders, in the words of Israeli commentator Aluf Benn, 'it looks like a border and behaves like one with barbed wire, electronic devices, concrete walls, watchtowers and checkpoints'.[3]

Then there was the circuitous course of the wall, which far from separating the incompatible populations left large numbers of Palestinian villagers and Israeli settlers on the 'wrong side'. If it was to serve as a border – which Israel still officially denies – why not build the wall along the armistice line of 1949, the internationally recognised Green Line? The 670-kilometre wall route – as opposed to the 315 kilometres of the Green Line – meant a proportionate rise in cost and in the time spent in construction, which seemed at odds with the project's paramount objective of saving lives. Furthermore, why did a route supposedly designed to prevent Palestinians from infiltrating Israel leave tens of thousands of potential assailants on the 'Israeli side' of the wall, with no physical obstacle to prevent them from entering Israel?[4]

In reality, the primary purpose of the wall is not security: in the words of UN Special Rapporteur John Dugard, 'what we are presently witnessing in the West Bank is a visible and clear act of territorial annexation under the guise of security'.[5] Specifically, the route was designed for the *de facto* annexation to Israel of the major settlement blocs, which had been implanted throughout the West Bank and East Jerusalem in contravention of international law. Furthermore, the wall took in not only the existing built-up areas of these settlements but abundant land and water reserves for their future expansion. Indeed, according to the Israeli human rights organisation B'Tselem, 'not only were security-related reasons of secondary importance in certain locations, in cases where they conflicted with settlement expansion, the planners opted for expansion, even at the price of compromised security'.[6]

These latest land expropriations and restriction on access to land and water resources come as no surprise to the Palestinians affected. After all, they had experienced expulsion and dispossession in 1948 and in 1967, and a determined campaign by Israel since the 1967 occupation to expropriate much of the West Bank as 'state land'. The introduction to this book places the wall and the disengagement from Gaza in their historical context as the latest attempts by Israel to manage its intractable 'native problem'. Both initiatives are ultimately driven by Prime Minister Sharon's recognition that territorial expansion must come to terms with the demographic realities of a superior Palestinian birth rate.

Chapter 1 outlines the background to the decision to build a wall. Although born of genuine security concerns, the route was ultimately determined by Sharon and settler interests. Subsequent pressure, both domestic and international, has led to a less intrusive route but the wall still joins the major settlement blocs to Israel, in addition to enclosing large tracts of the West Bank's most fertile land and productive water resources. Although it constitutes a new border there is no indication, however, that the wall marks the final frontier or that Israel's territorial designs are confined to the 10 per cent of the West Bank annexed *de facto*.

Success for the settlers' choice of route meant disaster for Palestinian communities cut off from families, clinics and schools in 'closed zones', as well as for the thousands of farmers whose access to lands, crops and water supplies depends on a restrictive and arbitrary gate and permit regime. Chapter 2 examines the devastating effect that the routing of the wall around Alfei Menashe settlement has inflicted on the city of Qalqilya and surrounding Palestinian communities. While wall-protected Israeli settlements thrive, the fear is that these

Palestine communities will wither away, deprived of land and livelihoods and the opportunity for future growth.

Chapter 3 focuses on East Jerusalem, where the wall represents the most significant alteration to the physical and political landscape since its capture and annexation by Israel in 1967. The route has been designed to improve the 'demographic balance' of Jews vis-à-vis Arabs, taking in the Jewish settlements in East Jerusalem and the annexed environs while 'walling out' densely populated Palestinian areas. Many Jerusalem Palestinians have already moved to the Israeli side through fear of losing residency and social service benefits, adding to the poverty and overcrowding in Arab localities, already heavily under-resourced in terms of infrastructure and public services. East Jerusalem remains the political, religious and cultural centre for Palestinians and the site of their future capital, and unilateral changes to its status bodes ill for a two-state solution or for a peaceful resolution to the conflict.

As detailed in Chapter 4, the high point of international opposition to the wall was the advisory opinion delivered by the International Court of Justice in July 2004. The ICJ not only ruled that the route violated international law but reaffirmed the illegality of settlements, while underscoring the link between the settlements and the 'sinuous route'. Although Israel, with US backing, ignored the injunction to cease construction and to dismantle the sections already built, there were concerns that non-compliance would lead to international sanctions, particularly on the part of the European Union. That Israeli fears came to naught was primarily due to Sharon's initiative to disengage unilaterally from Gaza. This, in the words of UN Special Rapporteur John Dugard, 'allowed Israel to continue with construction of the wall in Palestinian territory, the expansion of settlements and the de-Palestinization of Jerusalem with virtually no criticism'.[7] Indeed, such was the reversal of fortune that by mid-2005 Israel had been elected to the vice-presidency of the UN General Assembly, the same body which a year earlier had demanded without success that Israel comply with the ICJ advisory opinion.

With the international community largely failing the Palestinians with respect to the wall, it has mainly been left to local activists, international solidarity organizations and progressive Israelis to muster opposition. Veteran Israeli peace campaigner Uri Avnery spent the eve of his 82nd birthday in the village of Bil'in where 'the regular percussion of stun grenades and tear gas canisters was a background music'.[8] As Chapter 5 reveals, in other wall-threatened communities non-violent protests were met with more lethal force, resulting in Palestinian fatalities and injuries to their Israeli and international supporters. Nevertheless, non-violent activism continues in the face of Israeli repression of such protests and the international community's reluctance to ensure compliance with the ICJ advisory opinion.

In defiance of international law, the Bush administration has informed Israel that the United States will support Israel's retention of the main settlement blocs in any final peace agreement with the Palestinians. While these settlements prosper, secure behind the new border and enjoying direct territorial contiguity to Israel proper, Palestinian villages suffer under a regime of 'closed zones', gates and permits. This most recent dispossession has consequences beyond the local level, in that the 'amputation of Palestinian territory by the wall seriously interferes with the right of self-determination of the Palestinian people as it substantially reduces the size of the self-determination unit (already small) within which that right is to be exercised'.[9] Should the wall remain along its current land-grabbing route, this will sound the death knell for a meaningful two-state solution, leading instead to a Palestinian 'state' of separated cantons, devoid of territorial, political or economic integrity and lacking East Jerusalem as its capital.

NOTES

1. Gush Shalom, 'Replanting the olive trees of Jayyous', December 2004 <http://www.geocities.com/keller_adam/Replanting_the_trees_of_ Jayyous.htm/> (accessed on 21 October 2005).
2. Israel Ministry of Defence, *The Seam Zone* <http://www.seamzone. mod.gov.il/Pages/ENG/default.htm> (accessed on 21 October 2005).
3. Aluf Benn, 'Metamorphosis of Ariel Sharon', *Ha'aretz*, 17 August 2005.
4. The 'Israeli side' of the wall is still the West Bank for most of the route, and use of this term denotes a geographic position in relation to the wall, not a political designation.
5. *Question of the Violation of Human Rights in the Occupied Arab Territories, including Palestine: Report of the Special Rapporteur of the Commission on Human Rights, John Dugard, on the situation of human rights in the Palestinian territories occupied by Israel since 1967, to the Sixtieth session of the Commission on Human Rights, 8 September 2003*, para. 6. Available at <http://domino.un.org/unispal.nsf/0/8976be248c8e02ae85 256db1004dd7cc?OpenDocument> (accessed on 21 October 2005).
6. B'Tselem joint report with Bimkom, *Under the Guise of Security: Routing the Separation Barrier to Enable Israeli Settlement Expansion in the West Bank*, Summary, September 2005. <http://www.btselem.org/ English/Publications/Summaries/200509_Under_the_Guise_of_ Security.asp> (accessed on 18 October 2005).
7. *Israeli Practices Affecting the Human Rights of the Palestinian People in the Occupied Palestinian Territory, including East Jerusalem, 18 August 2005*, Summary. Available at <http://domino.un.org/unispal.nsf/ 9a798adbf322aff38525617b006d88d7/02bf82d785fe854a85257088004 c374c!OpenDocument> (accessed on 18 October 2005).
8. Uri Avnery, 'An odd birthday party', 10 September 2005, <http:// usa.mediamonitors.net/layout/set/print/content/view/full/19349> (accessed on 18 October 2005).
9. Dugard, *Question of the Violation of Human Rights in the Occupied Arab Territories, including Palestine*, 8 September 2003, para. 15. Available at <http://domino.un.org/unispal.nsf/0/8976be248c8e02ae85256db1004dd 7cc?OpenDocument> (accessed on 21 October 2005).

Acronyms

ACRI	Association for Civil Rights in Israel
ECHO	European Humanitarian Aid Office
GDP	gross domestic product
HEPG	Humanitarian and Emergency Policy Group
ICJ	International Court of Justice
IDF	Israeli Defence Forces
LACC	Local Aid Coordination Committee
NIS	new Israeli shekels
OCHA	*see* UNOCHA
PA	Palestinian Authority
PASSIA	Palestinian Academic Society for the Study of International Affairs
PENGON	Palestinian Environmental NGO Network
PSPB	Palestinian state 'with provisional borders'
TPS	town planning scheme
UN	United Nations
UNICEF	UN Children's Fund
UNOCHA	United Nations Office for the Coordination of Humanitarian Affairs
UNRWA	UN Relief and Works Agency for Palestine Refugees
UNSCO	Office of the Special Coordinator for the Peace Process in the Middle East
WCC	World Council of Churches
YESHA	Israeli settlers' council
dunam	unit of land measurement used in Palestine; one-quarter acre or 1,000 square metres

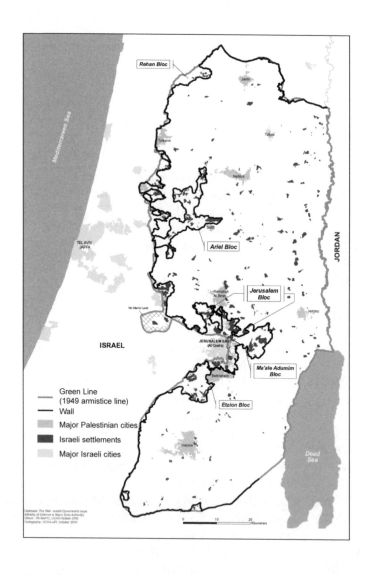

Map 1. Route of the wall approved by the Israeli cabinet,
February 2005

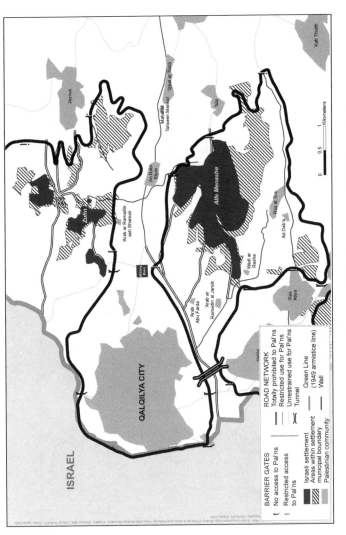

Map 2. The route of the wall in the western Qalqilya district

BARRIER GATES
⌐ No access to Pal'ns

╫ Restricted access
  to Pal'ns

ROAD NETWORK
Totally prohibited to Pal'ns
Restricted use for Pal'ns
Unrestrained use for Pal'ns
Tunnel

— Green Line
  (1949 armistice line)
— Wall

▨ Israeli settlement
▨ Areas within settlement
  municipal boundary
▨ Palestinian community

ISRAEL

QALQILYA CITY

Jayyous

Zufin

'Arab ar Ramadin
ash Shamali

An Nabi
Elyas

Mahattat
Tahseen Manhur

Izbat al Tabib

Isla

Alfe Menashe

'Arab
Abu Farda

'Arab ar
Ramadin al Janub

Habla

Ras at Tira

Ad Dab'a

Wadi ar
Rasha

Ras
Atiya

Kafr Thulth

0   0.5   1
Kilometers

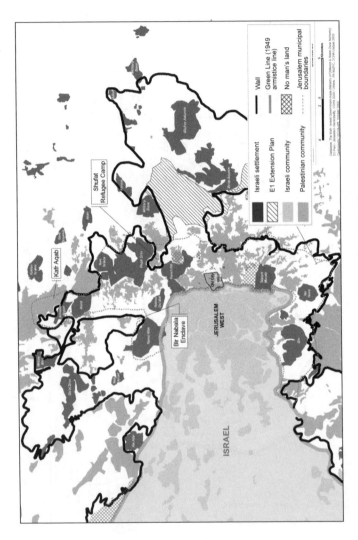

Map 3. The 'Jerusalem Envelope'

Legend:
- Israeli settlement
- E1 Extension Plan
- Israeli community
- Palestinian community
- Wall
- Green Line (1949 armistice line)
- No man's land
- Jerusalem municipal boundaries

Labels on map: Shufat Refugee Camp, Kafr Aqab, Bir Nabala Enclave, JERUSALEM WEST, ISRAEL

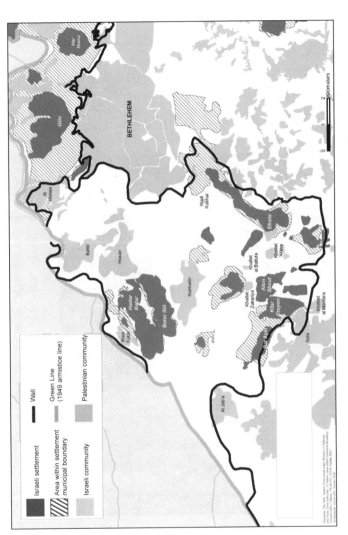

Map 4. Gush Etzion Settlement Bloc – Bethlehem district

Israeli settlement

Area within settlement
municipal boundary

Israeli community

Wall

Green Line
(1949 armistice line)

Palestinian community

Har
Homa

Gilo

BETHLEHEM

Al
Walaja

Battir

Husan

Nahalin

Wadi
Fukin

Hadar
Betar

Betar Illit

Khallet
Zakariya

Kfar
Etzyon

Alon
Shvut

Bat Ayin

Khallet
al Baltura

Wad
Rahhal

Efrata

Khallet
'Afana

Khirbet
al Manfara

Safa

Al Jab'a

0 1 2
Kilometers

Two children at Ma'sha, West Bank, whose house is now isolated in a 'closed zone' between the Wall and the settlement of Elkanna

Introduction

By Graham Usher

In June 2002 Israel's then Defence Minister, Binyamin Ben-Eliezer, cut the ribbon on the first phase of the West Bank wall near the Israeli village of Salem. Over the next three years the wall ploughed south, swerving eastwards into the West Bank to take in Jewish settlements on or near the Green Line, the armistice border established in 1949 at the end of the first Arab-Israeli war. It then cut a sweeping arc around the north, east and south of Palestinian East Jerusalem, occupied by Israel in 1967 at the end of the second Arab-Israeli war. Eventually it rejoined the Green Line east of Bethlehem and south of the Gush Etzion settlement bloc, repossessed in 1967 (Gush Etzion had been a small Jewish colony prior to the 1948 war).

The wall has been built ostensibly as a response to the second or al Aqsa *intifada*, the Palestinians' second national revolt in less than a decade and their third since Jewish immigrants began colonising their land in the late nineteenth century. The wall's route, impact, legality and significance are the subject of this book. The purpose of this introduction is to place the wall in the continuum of that history and to outline the future it augurs for Israel–Palestine, the most protracted, implacable and dangerous conflict of our time.

THE 'NATIVE PROBLEM'

Settler-colonial or settler-immigrant societies must fulfil four conditions if they are to survive. They must obtain a measure of political, military and economic independence from their metropolitan sponsors. They must achieve military hegemony over, or at least normal relations with, their neighbouring states. They must acquire international legitimacy. And they must resolve their 'native problem'.

Israel has been successful with the first three conditions. Between 1917 and 1947 the Zionist movement in Palestine wrested political, economic and military autonomy from Britain, the then imperial patron. It sealed its national independence through what remains the Zionist movement's greatest diplomatic achievement, aside from the 1917 Balfour Declaration: the UN partition plan of 29 November 1947, which recognised Israel as a Jewish state in 56.47 per cent of British Mandate Palestine. In 1967 it extended this victory by extracting retroactive legal recognition, courtesy of UN Resolution 242, for its military conquests in 1949 of a further 22 per cent of Mandate Palestine.

In the years since, Israel has forged a strategic – indeed paramount – relationship with the United States, now the world's sole military superpower. Securing Israel's existence and 'qualitative military edge' over its neighbours is now entrenched as one of the two pillars of US Middle East policy: access, protection and control of energy supplies in the Gulf being the other. Due to this absolute support, Israel has become the region's incontestable power. Its economy is three times larger than the combined economies of Egypt, Jordan, Lebanon, Syria and the Palestinian Authority. It is the world's fourth largest nuclear power (and the only one in the region), and the world's fifth largest arms exporter. By common assent (even of its adversaries), its armed forces are unmatched and unmatchable in the region. Whatever other attributes of independence Israel may lack (such as recognised borders), existential security is not among them, nor is international recognition of its existence as a Jewish state behind its 1949 armistice lines, or Green Line.

Because of this overarching power and legitimacy, Israel has consolidated its existence as a state without having to make a comprehensive peace agreement with its Arab neighbours or return the bulk of the territories it conquered from the Palestinians and Syrians in the 1948 and 1967 wars. On the contrary, it has achieved a degree of integration in the region, signing peace treaties with two Arab countries, Egypt and Jordan, and forging military ties with Turkey and, prior to its 1979 revolution, Iran.

Most remarkably of all, Israel has extracted submission from its primary victims, the Palestinians, who in 1988 and again in 1996 and 1998 accepted Israel behind its 1949 armistice lines and so renounced all sovereign claims to 78 per cent of what had been their ancestral homeland, including that allotted to 'the Arab state' in the 1947 UN partition plan. As others have remarked, this is an unprecedented concession in the annals of twentieth-century anti-colonial movements.[1]

But Israel has not solved its native problem and, as a result, has not yet fully achieved the other three conditions. As long as it is in latent or open conflict with the Palestinians and other front-line countries like Syria and Lebanon – and second-line powers like Iran – Israel will remain a garrison state, dependent on US military aid and diplomatic support and so vulnerable to changes in US policy. And as long as the Palestinians are not independent, Israel may be a secure state but it will not be accepted in the eyes of the peoples of the region or in the larger Muslim world – what used to be known as the Third World – or, increasingly, in Europe.

There is an irony here, for in 1949 the newly born Jewish state had more or less solved its native problem. As Israeli historian Baruch Kimmerling noted, the Zionist 'miracle' of the 1948 war was not only the expansion of Israel's territories far beyond the borders allocated to it in the 1947 UN partition plan. It was that these territories were almost entirely cleansed of their Palestinian inhabitants and their society deliberately destroyed, precisely to prevent their return and its rehabilitation. Kimmerling calls this act 'politicide'. He believes it to be a constant in Zionist policy and practice.[2]

In what was at least a partially premeditated military plan, beginning in March 1948, Israeli armed forces and Jewish militias razed some 400 Palestinian villages and towns, expelling or forcing the flight of some 750,000 people. The 100,000 or so Palestinians who remained within the Jewish state were, for the next 18 years, subject to martial law, alienated from their land and concentrated into small pales within Israel, mainly the Negev and Galilee. Their isolation was rendered complete through massive Jewish immigration: initially by Jewish survivors from the Nazi death camps, then by Jews from Arab countries and, after 1967, from countries in what was then the Soviet Union. On the eve of the 1967 war, the '1948 Palestinians' had become what Zionism had long deemed they should be: an unrecognised national minority in their own land.

Even in hindsight, Israel's accomplishments between 1947 and 1949 were stunning. Prior to the 1948 war, Jewish public agencies and private investors owned less than 7 per cent of the land of Palestine. Palestinians, individually or communally, owned 90 percent, of which 85 per cent belonged to the villages and towns that were later destroyed. Today – including the territories Israel occupied in the 1967 war – those figures, that ownership, are almost precisely reversed.

Yet having solved its native problem in 1948, Israel created it anew in 1967 when, in the course of the Six-Day War, it conquered Gaza, the West Bank, East Jerusalem, the Egyptian Sinai and the Syrian Golan Heights. Once more, Israel had charge of over a million non-Jewish Arabs, and once more it was confronted with the dilemma of what to do with them. Over time four options emerged.

a) Israel could annex the occupied territories without granting citizenship to the Palestinians, resolving its native problem through a colonial apartheid regime of South African vintage.
b) Alternatively, it could annex the territories but grant citizenship to Palestinians, ending the native problem by replacing Israel's exclusivist or ethnic sectarian character as a Jewish state with an inclusive, non-sectarian and unitary 'state for all its citizens'.
c) It could offer to withdraw from the territories, which would form a Palestinian state in the West Bank and Gaza, in return for Arab recognition of Israel as 'the democratic state of the Jewish people'.
d) It could repeat the 1948 experience by cleansing Palestinians from the West Bank and Gaza or those parts deemed vital to Israel's military, demographic and territorial ambitions.

The wall represents a compromise between those choices. It attempts to escape the opprobrium that a) would incur, or the end of the Zionist project posited by b), by imposing a final settlement on the Palestinians made up of an amalgam of c) and d).

SEPARATION

In contrast to 1948 – when the expulsion of Palestinians from their lands had been hidden and/or justified by the imperatives of war and Jewish survival – there was no Israeli consensus, post-1967, over the fate of the newly acquired territories. The nationalist and increasingly messianic right argued for annexation and transfer: the natives would either be spirited across the border as in 1948 or remain as 'resident aliens' in their homeland. What became known as the Israeli peace camp argued for a more or less full withdrawal, although more to preserve Jewish ethnic and religious hegemony inside Israel 'proper' than out of any genuinely anti-colonialist sentiment.

The mainstream Zionist parties, Labour and Likud, drew rhetorically on both positions but practised neither. The preference was to defer all options, first through the fiction that there was no Palestinian people, then through the fiction there was no Palestinian partner. They pursued policies of neither formal annexation nor withdrawal but rather of *de facto*, creeping annexation and the induced transfer of Palestinians from areas that one or the other or both parties sought to keep for Israel. Both Labour and Likud originally held common territorial and/or ideological objectives – the annexation of an expanded East Jerusalem being one. But the longer the occupation lasted (and the more Palestinian resistance to it grew), the more Labour opted for a territorial compromise, even, ultimately, in East Jerusalem; and the more Likud accepted the need for a demographic compromise, also, ultimately, in East Jerusalem.

For both, however, the central instrument for conquest and annexation – as it had been in the pre-state Zionist movement and within Israel – was Jewish colonial settlement and the alienation of Palestinian land. Under the Labour-led governments of 1968–77, the rationale behind settlement and expropriation was strategic and defensive. Some 30 settlements were established around East Jerusalem and the 'extremities' of the Jordan Valley, Golan Heights and southern Gaza Strip, all more or less to create a buffer between the Palestinians and their Arab hinterlands.

After the election of Menachem Begin's Likud coalition in 1977 – in alliance with the new, nationalist, messianic settler movement, Gush Emunim – the rationale was ideological and preemptive. Likud implanted settlements deep in the mountainous regions of the central West Bank. These ranges were the living artery of the six main Palestinian cities of Jenin, Nablus, Ramallah, East Jerusalem, Bethlehem and Hebron: the spine of any future West Bank Palestinian state.

These conquests were couched in terms of Biblical redemption, but the goal was straightforwardly colonial: creating geographic and demographic facts in the heart of the West Bank to entrench the Jewish position and break the back of a coherent Palestinian entity. 'The aim is to render it difficult for the minority [sic] Arab population to unite and create territorial and political continuity,' wrote Matityahu Drobles in his 1978 *Master Plan for the Development of Judea and Samaria*, the blueprint for Likud's settlement project. The plan called for the establishment of 125 settlements in the West Bank, with the aim of transplanting a million Jews there by the year 2000.

Israel has yet to reach that target. But the infrastructure for such a demographic and geographic 'second' transformation of Palestine is in place. It is being realised through policies ominously similar to the first transformation in 1948.

Today over 400,000 Jewish settlers live in East Jerusalem and the West Bank in 137 settlements and 100 more 'outposts' that may become the nuclei of future settlements. These colonies have regional and municipal control of over 40 per cent of all West Bank territory, with a further 30 per cent earmarked as potential land reserves and/or security zones. They are integrated legally, spatially, culturally and materially into Israel through laws, services, infrastructure and a road network that reaches all the way from Tel Aviv to the Jordan River. Theirs is the colonial settler state: 'it is all Israel,' as one army reservist put it to this writer outside one of the wall gates. By circumventing and isolating the Palestinian areas, this same state consigns 2.4 million Palestinians to a series of disconnected cantons – these are their homeland or 'homelands', none of them Palestine.

Israel's relations with its new post-1967 Palestinian 'minority' mirrored those it had developed with their 1948 brethren. First of all there was ethnic cleansing. Some 300,000 Palestinians have been expelled from the occupied territories, most during the 1967 war but others subsequently, including some of the Palestinians' ablest political leaders. There has been martial law. Some 650,000 men (40 per cent of the Palestinian male population) have been imprisoned in the last 38 years, overwhelmingly for nationalist offences, many without charge or trial. And there has been displacement or induced transfer, not only through mammoth land expropriations to clear the way for settlement in the West Bank but also through the destruction of over 12,000 Palestinian homes in areas taken by Israel.

Where all else failed, there was violent suppression, particularly during periods when Palestinians moved from passive resistance to active revolt. In the second *intifada* (the bloodiest rebellion inside Palestine since Israel's establishment), Israeli soldiers and settlers have killed 3,000 Palestinians, including 1,600 not involved in hostilities. Over the same period, 1,000 Israelis have been killed, over 400 of them civilian casualties of Palestinian suicide attacks inside Israel.

In this continuing conflict, and given the lack of a Zionist consensus over the 1967 territories, neither genocide nor wholesale transfer nor continued, overpowering violence was a real option for Israel – save perhaps in scenarios of existential threat. And as then Israeli Prime Minister, Ehud Barak, admitted in

1999, the Palestinians never constituted an existential threat to Israel. 'The Palestinians are the source of legitimacy for the continuation of the conflict,' he said. 'But as a military threat they are ludicrous.'

Instead – and especially in the 'quiet' decades between the 1967 conquest and the first 1987 *intifada* – Israel's main policy was to disintegrate Palestinian society in the occupied territories by partially integrating its remnants into Israel's own. Combined with military rule, 'partial integration' was supposed to create such levels of political, social and economic dependency between Israel and the Palestinians that the possibility of political and economic sovereignty was annulled and, with it, aspirations to national independence.

Dependency was achieved: by 1987 all aspects of Palestinian civilian life (from schoolbooks to car ownership) in the occupied territories were controlled by Israel and the Palestinian economy was organically tied to the Israel's, with over 200,000 Palestinians working in or for their occupier's service on any one day. But Palestinian nationalism did not fade; it grew.

The catalyst for this was the 1969 takeover of the Palestine Liberation Organization by Palestinian guerrilla factions, first and foremost Yasser Arafat's Fatah movement. Despite its failures to liberate the land, first in 1948 and again in 1967, the PLO under Arafat's leadership scored three successes. It united a dispersed people under the aegis of one 'sole' national liberation movement. It steered international attention to a national (as opposed to a humanitarian) cause that, prior to 1969, had been ignored or, in Israel's case, denied. And it disseminated a modern national consciousness based on self-determination and return that took root wherever Palestinians resided, including the occupied territories. It also – with Arafat the prime steward – gradually established a new national consensus based on the recognition of Israel behind the Green Line and an independent Palestinian state in Gaza and the West Bank, with (East) Jerusalem as its capital.

The florescence of that new national consciousness came in 1987 when Palestinians, in their thousands, took to the streets of the occupied territories (but not in Israel or the diaspora) in open revolt against their masters. Israel's inability to do anything other than contain what was an overwhelmingly civilian, popular and nationalist uprising (not to speak of the ignominy caused by televised images of the region's mightiest army quelling the revolt by breaking the bones of unarmed youths) brought a revision to the Labour–Likud consensus: 'no withdrawal, no annexation but no *status quo ante* either', in the phrase of Palestinian intellectual Azmi Bishara.[3]

From then on partial integration was replaced with policies of ethnic separation, as direct military rule gave way to neo-colonial prescriptions based on indirect military control and limited Palestinian autonomy. These formulae were to come to fruition with the 1992 Labour coalition government of Yitzhak Rabin, the 1993 Oslo accords and their offspring, the Palestinian Authority (PA).

As Bishara commented at the time, the PA is a unique polity in the annals of political science: 'it is an autonomy for non-citizens', in which the PA has many of the civilian functions of government but none of a state's attributes of legal, territorial, political or military sovereignty. Those prerogatives remained Israel's: the sole 'sovereign' power in the occupied territories by virtue of its ability to dictate and control all aspects of Palestinian life and development.

That the PA's existence amounted to even a 'limited autonomy' in the occupied territories was a moot point, finally rendered irrelevant by Israel's re-conquest of the PA 'controlled' West Bank cities in 2002 and increasingly ruthless invasions of Gaza thereafter. But the notion of separation based on race or ethnicity was becoming real.

It began during the first Gulf War under Yitzhak Shamir's Likud government. This cancelled the Palestinians 'general exit permit' into Israel. Hitherto – as part of the integration policy – Palestinians from the occupied territories (except for those deemed security risks) had enjoyed freedom of movement inside Israel. After 1991 a blanket ban was imposed on Palestinian mobility into Israel save for those with special 'passes': workers, merchants, humanitarian cases, collaborators and, with the establishment of the PA, VIPs (a class stratification that was to cause enormous Palestinian resentment during the Oslo years). Separation was made possible by the Israeli economy shifting from labour-intensive to capital-intensive production, and by the import of foreign migrant workers to do the 'guest-worker' jobs once allotted to Palestinians from the territories.

Separation deepened under Yitzhak Rabin's Labour government. In 1993 – following the first *intifada*'s final resort to armed struggle – he imposed a 'general closure' on the occupied territories, segregating Gaza from the West Bank and both from occupied East Jerusalem. This became formalised under Oslo with the erection of an electronic fence around the Gaza Strip and spatial 'ethnic' divisions within it: Israeli-controlled military/settlement areas cover around 20 per cent of all territory (including the border), with the remainder hosting some 1.3 million Palestinians and eight refugee camps, under the PA's charge.

In the West Bank the division was even more Kafkaesque and racially stratified: the PA had civilian and security control in around 18 per cent of the West Bank, divided into eight disconnected urban areas, and civilian control in 22 percent, again internally divided but containing most Palestinian villages and hamlets. Israel had exclusive control over the rest of the intervening territory (including of course East Jerusalem), hosting fewer than 100,000 Palestinians but containing vast land reserves for settlement expansion and security zones.

This was the territorial and demographic segmentation which the Labour Prime Minister, Shimon Peres, activated in 1996 following a wave of Hamas and Islamic Jihad suicide bombings in Israel. Enforcing the system through the construction of Jewish-only bypass roads and strategically located army bases, Peres not only isolated the West Bank and Gaza Strip one from the other, but also instituted a system of 'internal closure' that separated villages from towns and people from their neighbours, fields and orchards.

Ostensibly this was to secure the settlements, but its primary purpose was to surround and sever each Palestinian locality, tearing apart the basic sinews of Palestinian society. Its political purpose was to act as the most brutal leverage on the PA. And it worked. Following the imposition of the internal closure, Arafat arrested 1,200 Islamist 'suspects' and shut down Hamas-controlled mosques and welfare associations. Clearly the Palestinian leader had seen the future. (The same leverage was employed following the outbreak of the second *intifada* in 2000, and for the same purpose. But this time Arafat refused the role of satrap.)

It was around this time that the idea of a separation wall began to emerge. In 1995 – in one of his last acts as prime minister – Rabin commissioned the then Energy Minister, Moshe Shahal, to design a 'security fence' more or less paralleling the West Bank Green Line. At the height of the 1996 crisis, Peres approved the construction of a 2-kilometre wide 'buffer zone' along the Green Line comprising fences, electronic surveillance fields, helicopter patrols and a permanent presence of soldiers and police, all to prevent Palestinian entry into Israel.[4] His successor, Likud Prime Minister Binyamin Netanyahu, shelved the plan, wary that a security border along the Green Line might be mistaken for a political one.

It was taken up again by Labour Prime Minister Ehud Barak when, at Camp David in July 2000, he finally sat down with the Palestinian leadership to negotiate a final status agreement. Like Rabin and Peres, Barak preferred a negotiated solution since 'the Palestinians are the source of legitimacy for a continuation of the conflict'. He wanted the consent testified by Arafat's signature. But consent was to be buttressed by US pressure and Israeli coercion, made possible by the existing realities of settlement, the closure regime in the occupied territories and the future threat of a wall to defend them.

In exchange for Israel's withdrawal from around 90 per cent of the West Bank and all of Gaza, Barak sought Palestinian acceptance for Israel's annexation of three major West Bank settlement blocs (Ariel, Maale Adumim and Gush Etzion), all of the settlements in occupied East Jerusalem and a more or less permanent Israeli military presence in the eastern West Bank. Had this been the final deal, it would certainly have alleviated the weight of Israel's occupation of the West Bank and Gaza, but would not have ended Israel's overall control of them. This is what Arafat foresaw and why – despite the inordinate American pressure – he hesitated to sign the 'peace of the brave'.

Camp David ultimately foundered on the rock of Jewish and Palestinian sovereignty on or under the Haram Al Sharif/ Temple Mount in occupied East Jerusalem, as well as Barak's refusal to tolerate any meaningful solution for the Palestinian refugees. Having 'torn the mask off' Palestinian irredentism, Barak then proceeded to 'unilateral separation': the imposition of Israel's final borders, based on a separation wall annexing those occupied territories Israel sought to keep in the West Bank combined with an un-negotiated withdrawal from those deemed expendable, especially the Gaza Strip.

In November 2000 – one month into the second *intifada* – Barak authorised the building of a 'barrier to prevent the passage of motor vehicles' in the northern end of the West Bank. In June 2001 – under a domestic clamour to end Palestinian suicide bombings – his successor as premier, Ariel Sharon, asked the National Security Director and Barak loyalist, Uzi Dayan, to formulate measures that would prevent Palestinians from infiltrating into Israel. Dayan's fundamental recommendation was that a permanent barrier be built along the length of the border, a plan similar to those of Peres in 1996 and Barak in 2000. Within a month, the plan received cabinet endorsement. One year later Ben-Eliezer (another Barak protege) cut the ribbon at Salem.

For the Palestinians, schooled in the imposed realities of the settlements, the closure regime and 'autonomy', the wall was less the abandonment of Oslo than its logical, if terrifying, outcome. For Israel's political class the consecration of the wall – and the failure of the negotiated solution it signified – marked a posthumous victory for the 'iron wall' revisionism of Zeev Jabotinsky. This is a doctrine that does not abandon the goal of a final Israeli-Palestinian agreement. It simply insists that it must follow (rather than precede) Israel's final, unilateral determination of its own borders.

'The sole way to such an agreement is through the iron wall, that is to say, the establishment in Palestine of a force that will in no way be influenced by Arab pressure,' wrote Jabotinsky in 1923. 'In other words, the only way to achieve a settlement in the future is total avoidance of all attempts to arrive at a settlement in the present.'[5]

THE DEMOGRAPHIC WALL

Sharon was a reluctant convert to the wall, and even more to the actual, political partition the wall foreshadows within the West Bank. Throughout his political career he had been a territorial expansionist, the champion of Greater Israel: his plan was that of Drobles, who drew it up under Sharon's guidance as Begin's Agricultural Minister. Yet in February 2005 the prime minister approved a route that more or less mirrors the map Barak presented to the Palestinians at Camp David, and which he had then denounced as a mortal threat to Israel's existence. What changed his mind? One reason was that despite three years of unprecedented repression – including Israel's restitution of direct martial rule throughout the West Bank – Sharon had failed to crush the second *intifada* by military means.

However disproportionate the scale of the two people's suffering, the *intifada* was hurting the Israeli economy, widening fractures in Israeli society and weakening the consensus Sharon had manufactured behind his militarist solutions. One of the reasons for the popular demand for a wall was the Israeli public's weariness with a 'normal' reality that combined sporadic suicide attacks in Israel with continuous, low-intensity guerrilla warfare in the occupied territories. In 2002 over 1,000 reservists refused to serve 'in a war for the settlements' in the occupied territories. Elite air force corps ('Really, our finest young people', in the words of Sharon's advisor, Dov Weisglass[6]) said no to aerial assassination missions, especially when the target was embedded in densely populated Palestinian cities.

There was also donor fatigue. The international community had been prepared to support the PA to the tune of US$1 billion a year as long as there was at least the fiction of a peace process. But in the aftermath of the West Bank re-conquest and the punitive regime that kept it in place, by 2003 the truth of ongoing occupation could no longer be denied. Certain international aid organizations (in particular, the International Committee of the Red Cross) questioned whether their mandates included shoring up a deliberately pauperised people, given that Israel as the occupying power was responsible for the welfare of those under occupation under international law.

There were also political alternatives emerging to Sharon's non-solutions of military repression and 'interim agreements' of indefinite duration. In 2003 the United States came up with the Road Map peace plan. Sharon accepted its first phase, with sequenced political progress on Palestinian reform and the 'fight against terror'. But he was alarmed by the third, with its call for a return to final status negotiations that would 'end the occupation that began in 1967'. He accurately foresaw the bases on which those negotiations would rest.

In 2002 – in arguably the most important Arab initiative in 50 years of conflict – the 22 member states of the Arab League offered 'full normalisation' in return for Israel's full withdrawal from the 1967 occupied territories and an 'agreed' resolution of the refugee problem (a proviso that essentially gives Israel veto power over the extent of refugee return). In 2003 an unofficial peace process between former Israeli and Palestinian negotiators produced the Geneva Accord, a 'virtual' agreement in which Israel withdraws from 98 per cent of the West Bank and accepts Palestinian sovereignty over Arab areas in East Jerusalem in return for the Palestinians' practical renunciation of the right of return. Sharon eluded the Arab initiative by reinvading the West Bank; he evaded Geneva by declaring a unilateral withdrawal from Gaza and accelerating construction of the wall.

But the fundamental imperative driving Sharon's separation plan was neither political nor military; it was once again the 'native problem'. Today there are approximately 10 million people living in the Israeli-controlled territories between the Mediterranean Sea and Jordan River, with a slight Jewish majority. By 2012 there will be parity with the Palestinian Arabs. By 2025 Palestinians will be the majority. As a state predicated on ethnic supremacy, this is the only real existential threat that the Jewish state faces. And it has brought forth in Sharon radical responses. It is, for example, the only meaningful rationale behind Sharon's plan to withdraw from the Gaza Strip.

Disengagement cannot be justified militarily, since it represents at least a partial victory for the Palestinian armed resistance and does nothing to prevent future attacks on neighbouring Israeli towns. Nor can it be understood as a 'first step' back to the Road Map. On the contrary (as Weisglass explained), the entire purpose of disengagement is to freeze the political process until the Palestinians become Finns (in other words, presumably, an inconceivably distant future) and accept a permanent or interim settlement on Israel's terms. Its only logic is demographic: the desperate fear that, unless it somehow ends its presence in Gaza, Israel will one day find itself responsible for its 1.3 million Palestinian residents.

Demography is also the rationale behind Israel's new naturalisation policies. These grant citizenship to any Jew on the planet, but place draconian restrictions on citizenship to any Palestinians in the occupied territories or elsewhere who marry their cousins inside Israel (in some cases, their actual cousins): in Kimmerling's phrase, this is a 'herrenvolk law' that is utterly unabashed about making ethnic discrimination and racial supremacy the cornerstone of policy. Plans are already in place to expel 'across the border' thousands of 'illegal' Palestinians now in Israel once the border – that is, the wall – is built.

It is demography that has dictated the course of the wall. In October 2003, the Israeli cabinet approved the first plan, drawn up by Sharon and his Defence Minister, Shaul Mofaz. This would have effectively annexed around 16 per cent of the West Bank, while leaving scores of settlements, outposts, military areas and 700 kilometres of Jewish-only roads beyond the wall to the east. For these to be defensible (in the opinion of Israeli cartographer Shaul Arieli), a wall or security zone along the Jordan Valley would be required.

The 2003 wall thus mirrors Sharon's 1975 master plan for the West Bank: an Israeli-annexed seam three to five kilometres wide east of the Green Line, and a 10 to 15-kilometre seam annexed west of the Jordan River. He called it then his Bantustan plan, since it concentrates the Palestinians into three disconnected enclaves or 'homelands': Jenin and Ramallah, with a corridor to Jericho; Bethlehem and Hebron; and Gaza, which would have no land corridor to the West Bank. Altogether it would leave Palestinians 53 per cent of a fragmented West Bank, with no claim or connection to East Jerusalem.

But there was one major problem with the plan, aside from the rulings of the International Court of Justice and the Israeli High Court, and disquiet from the United States. It incorporated 400,000 Palestinians on the 'Israeli side' of the wall, including 200,000 in East Jerusalem. Once again, driven by the colonial appetite to expand or retain territorial gains acquired by force, Israel was reproducing its own demographic risks.

The revised route approved by the cabinet in February 2005 provides only a partial remedy. It annexes 10 per cent of the West Bank, with 49,000 Palestinians on the Israeli side, mainly in villages north of Tulkarm, south of Qalqilya and west of Bethlehem. Through settlement expansion, restrictions on entry into Israel and isolation from PA services, the likelihood is that these enclaves will wither away. 'The rationale is to create the conditions for voluntary transfer so that the Palestinians will abandon their homes and go [east] to the big Palestinian cities,' argues Arieli. This will make it 'possible to expand the borders of Israel without paying the demographic price, because if you change the demography, you change the geography'.[7] Should the Palestinians prove resilient and remain on their land, another option in the future may be to exchange the 49,000 Palestinians on the 'Israeli' side of the wall for the approximately 70,000 Jewish settlers beyond it: a 'soft' transfer but a transfer nonetheless.

This is probably not Sharon's preferred solution. He has admitted that the 2005 route is inadequate from a security point of view: it leaves dozens of isolated settlements in fatal proximity to major Palestinian cities like Nablus. But to have included Nablus within the wall, Sharon concedes, would mean annexing 'hundreds of thousands of Palestinians who would eventually join up with the Israeli Arabs, and that would become a major problem.'[8] Demography, clearly, now trumps defence, including that of the settlements.

Another problem is that the February 2005 route still leaves 130,000 Palestinians within the wall being built around East Jerusalem. This is why few Israelis believe the 'Jerusalem Envelope' will stay in its present form: it is rather 'an interim security stage', admits Israel's former Shin Bet chief Avi Dichter (one of the strongest advocates for the wall). The likeliest revision will be to reroute the wall to exclude Palestinian neighbourhoods within annexed East Jerusalem, reducing the Palestinian Jerusalem presence still further, with the remnant mostly concentrated in and around the Old City. Given the sensitivities of trying to evict Palestinians – Muslim and Christian – from their holiest sites, this is probably a demographic problem Israel can live with, at least for now, especially if it is accompanied by increased Jewish settlement in and around Jerusalem's 'holy basin'.

Sharon, therefore, has not cynically hijacked notions of separation, Palestinian statehood and withdrawal from his

Labour rivals to conceal his old Greater Israel ambitions. On the contrary, he has become convinced by such notions. Like Israel's first prime minister, David Ben-Gurion, when faced with the 1947 partition plan, he has had to unpick the knot of 'the completeness of the land without a Jewish state or a Jewish state without the completeness of the land'. And, like Ben-Gurion, he has 'chosen a Jewish state without the completeness of land'.[9]

Like Jabotinsky, however, Sharon believes the borders of the incomplete land of Israel must be determined and imposed unilaterally, 'uninfluenced' by Arab pressure. For Sharon, the ultimate source of such pressure remains the Palestinian Authority, the international legitimacy it commands, and the national and legally sanctioned aspirations of self-determination, independence and return it represents. This is why the new Sharon – like the old – understands that the imposed solution requires, first, politicide: 'the dissolution of the Palestinian people's existence as a legitimate social, political and economic entity', in Kimmerling's definition.

During much of the second *intifada*, this involved the deliberate destruction of the PA as a centralised and national entity as well as the internationally successful demonisation of its elected leader, Yasser Arafat. Under the watch of Arafat's successor Mahmoud Abbas, 'Abu Mazen', it involves attrition: refusing to address Palestinian national aspirations by deferring any return to meaningful political negotiations; making political preconditions (such as the forcible disarmament of Palestinian militias) whose likeliest outcome would be a Palestinian civil war; and disintegrating the PA into its regional parts, with the first stage being the nurturing of a separate 'disengagement' administration in Gaza.

This does not necessarily entail the PA's absolute destruction, although that, in fact, may be the consequence. Sharon has no problem with the PA as a civil administration; on the contrary, its existence is necessary to take care of the material needs of the Palestinians. But he has an enormous problem with it being recognised, domestically and internationally, as a political and national authority, as the nucleus of a future Palestinian state, with East Jerusalem as its capital.

There is only one kind of Palestinian entity Sharon could accept. Its contours were outlined by him in December 2002 and inserted by him in George Bush's Middle East policy speech of June 2002: a Palestinian state 'with provisional borders' (PSPB). In return for 'statehood', he would demand that the PA postpone indefinitely all negotiation on final status issues: Jerusalem, settlements, borders, refugees, and water and other resources. This would represent an enormous strategic gain for Sharon. It would reduce for the foreseeable future the Israeli-Palestinian conflict to a Kashmir-like border dispute within the West Bank, while allowing him the time to consolidate Israel's demographic supremacy behind the wall and territorial and military control beyond it. In exchange for these advantages – and for staunch US backing – he may even be tempted to offer a further West Bank withdrawal, with between 17 and 23 isolated settlements being evacuated.

The PA's current position is to reject the PSPB unless accompanied by US and UN guarantees on the shape, parameters and timetable for a final agreement. If it holds to these conditions, Sharon will probably continue to act unilaterally, building an internal and international consensus around the settlement blocs on the 'Israeli' side of the wall while consolidating those West Bank 'blocs in embryo' (Elon Moreh, Shilo, Ofra, Beit El, Tekoa and Kiryat Arba) that currently lie beyond the wall but that connect the West Bank's western settlements to their eastern counterparts. Given Sharon's objectives, this would not foreclose the PSPB. Separation would still be ensured by a system throughout the West Bank of Palestinian-only roads, bridges, underpasses and tunnels. Palestinian contiguity would be 'transportational', not territorial. Israel would control all access to the last remaining urban and rural land reserves of these areas.

Whether imposed or negotiated – and whether it comprises 53 or 90 per cent of the West Bank – a PSPB remains totally consistent with Sharon and Drobles' 27-year-old master plan for preventing Palestinian 'territorial and political continuity'. It would reduce the PA's actual role to that of a vast municipality: a 'functional' payer of salaries and provider of services. This is why the state would necessarily be 'provisional', and not only because of the fluidity of its borders. Under these conditions, it could never be economically viable, politically independent, internally democratic or territorially sovereign. It would be a state doomed to politicide, not least for the lack of a leadership that would agree to it.

If this is the future – with all its implications for the hope of genuine Palestinian independence – what options do the Palestinians have? 'I can only see two,' says Bishara. 'First, the Jordanian option, in which what is left of Palestine integrates with the larger Jordanian sovereignty and so, in that way, returns to the Arab world. Second, in the struggle against the Bantustans, we pose as their alternative not statehood, but a binational state for the whole of Israel/Palestine.'[10]

Since Israel's entire purpose behind the policies of demographic separation, autonomy and the wall has been to prevent the 'nightmare' of a binational unitary state, it is unlikely that any foreseeable future Israeli (or US) government would accept the second solution – even a government made up of the Israeli peace camp (which historically was more committed to separation than Sharon).

This leaves the Jordanian option for the West Bank and, for Gaza, an Egyptian variation on the same, with the possibility of extending the Strip's land base south into the Sinai rather than north and east into Israel.[11] To regionalise – or, more precisely, denationalise – the question of Palestine is an ambition Sharon has long nurtured. One of the ulterior motives behind his unilateral war against Lebanon in 1982 was precisely to 'create the conditions' for a resolution of the Palestinian issue on the basis of the notion that Jordan is Palestine, i.e. that the Palestinians could set up their state in or instead of the Hashemite Kingdom of Jordan rather than in any part of historic Palestine. Twenty-three years on, he has revised this grand geo-political scheme in one significant way. He no longer believes that Jordan is Palestine, given the political and practical impossibility of a 1948-like decanting of the Palestinians across the river. Rather 'Palestine', or more precisely its West Bank and Gaza leftovers, will ultimately become annexes of Jordan and Egypt.

AGAINST THE WALL

Such a future would mean the liquidation of the Palestinian cause, if not as a rallying symbol, then as a practical project. Is there anything the Palestinians and their supporters around the world can do to resist it?

One strategy is that advocated by the new Palestinian president, Abu Mazen, and the greater part of the Palestinian leadership. This consists of implementing every reform the US demands of them – including, ultimately, the disarmament of the Palestinian militias – so that the PA can return to the Road Map. During its first phase, Abu Mazen will demand an end to all unilateral actions by Israel, including settlement expansion and the construction of the wall. From there – and as rapidly as possible – he wants to negotiate a final status agreement based on 'a combination of the Clinton parameters [issued in December 2000], the Taba negotiations, the Arab peace initiative and the Geneva Accord, and subject to a Palestinian referendum', says an aide.[12]

Should an agreement be worked out along these lines, the wall would be partially but not wholly dismantled, since these various agreements assume Israel's annexation of the Maale Adumim and Gush Etzion settlement blocs. The Palestinian leadership, however, would seek to prevent Maale Adumim and Ariel being physically incorporated by the wall. Needless to say, few Palestinian negotiators see a Geneva-like deal as a just solution to their cause, certainly in terms of what justice and international law grants them. But there are many – including, some say, Abu Mazen – who believe that Geneva or something similar represents the maximum of 'attainable justice' his people can achieve given Israel's overwhelming strength, the hegemony of its demographic discourse and the current international balance of power in its favour.

It remains to be seen whether the Palestinian people would be so defeatist as to vote in favour of a final peace deal that annuls the right of return for the Palestinian refugees, achieves nothing for the national status of the Palestinians in Israel, truncates and reduces Palestinian East Jerusalem, and isolates or displaces those Palestinians who live in or near those settlement areas annexed to Israel by the wall. But even if the Palestinians were to accept a Geneva-like deal, such a denouement assumes active intervention on the part of the United States. And US reluctance to press Israel to do anything it does not want to do increases with time. In fact, with the rise of the neo-conservative agendas of unilateralism, preemption and regime change, Washington has increasingly adopted Israel's neo-colonial stances as its own.

In April 2004 George Bush overturned 50 years of US policy positions – not to speak of the entire corpus of UN resolutions and international law – by backing Israel's insistence that: a) the right of return should be confined to an undefined Palestinian state in the West Bank and Gaza, and b) Israel would not be expected to withdraw from 'major population centers' (i.e. illegal settlement blocs) in the West Bank in any final peace agreement with the Palestinians.

Since then, Bush has accepted Sharon's dictum that the Gaza disengagement be seen as a unilateral Israeli action separate from the Road Map, and has refused Abu Mazen's plea to skip its interim stage of a PSPB in favour of an expedited return to final status talks. The belief, therefore, that Washington will actively intervene on Abu Mazen's behalf will almost certainly prove illusory. It is far more likely that the United States will intervene actively on Sharon's behalf to persuade the Palestinians to accept a PSPB, especially if oiled by the promise of a further Israeli West Bank withdrawal. For the PA this will almost certainly prove an interim agreement too far, given the absolute opposition to the PSPB by the Palestinian factions, including Abu Mazen's ruling Fatah movement. The more likely result of Abu Mazen's passive diplomacy will thus be a replay of the Oslo experience: a managed impasse leading to renewed confrontation with Israel and/or between the PA and the Palestinian people.

Should this imposed settlement come to pass, the Islamist movements of Hamas and Islamic Jihad, as well as the other Palestinian militias, may revive their strategy of armed struggle. This will consist not only of suicide attacks in Israel and guerrilla war in the occupied territories but also high-trajectory missiles to overcome and over-fly the wall. Auguries of this future can be seen in the mortar attacks the militias have employed against the settlements in Gaza and Israeli towns abutting Gaza's border.

Armed struggle is not an inevitable development. For now Hamas is observing a ceasefire and, say its leaders, is prepared to give negotiations and international diplomacy another chance to end the occupation. But three factors could bring about a revival of armed struggle. One is for Israel to resume its policy of assassinating Hamas and other Palestinian leaders. The second, which Palestinians fully expect, would be for Sharon to follow disengagement with accelerated and massive settlement and wall construction in the West Bank, and especially in and around East Jerusalem. The third would be if the PA were to renege on its commitment to hold parliamentary and further municipal elections throughout the occupied territories, fuelling Hamas's suspicions that Fatah is unable or unwilling to share power in a new 'reformed' Palestinian leadership.

Whatever its dubious success in Gaza, a mortar war in the West Bank is fraught with risk. It would incur massive Israeli retaliation, especially if the mortars fired over the wall were to reach cities within Israel proper. In the least case this would mean re-conquest, and the collapse of what remains of the PA as a government. In the worst, it could mean destruction and forced displacement, especially from villages and other areas whence the mortars were fired. It would grant Sharon the popular and diplomatic licence to further consolidate his hold on the West Bank, either through the establishment of even more expansive security zones around settlement blocs beyond the wall or through the construction of an eastern wall. Finally, it would further risk transforming the conflict from a territorial dispute to a religious one: this at least was the premonition of Faisal Husseini, the late and lamented PLO representative in Jerusalem.

'There are many forms of fundamentalism in our region – Islamic, Jewish and nationalist,' Husseini said, one month before the al Aqsa *intifada* erupted in September 2000. 'They have a lot of energy but no target, no rallying symbol. But were the peace process to collapse, Jerusalem would become the symbol and the target. And once that happens the only outcome is collision.'[13]

There is a third strategy that has yet to be tried, but that is alluded to in Chapters 4 and 5. It is also being mooted throughout the PA and the Palestinian factions, including Hamas, confronted by the unique challenges posed by the wall.

One such challenge is how to transform the PA from an administrative and largely absent 'authority' into a vanguard central power that is able to marshal and lead the immense mobilising potential of its people behind a mass, civil and non-violent movement against occupation – in other words, how to fashion the PA not only as an entity ready for statehood but also as an instrument for national liberation.

Few Palestinians have a clear answer, other than that democracy must be an integral part of the transformation. As Palestinian political analyst Khalil Shikaki has said, free and fair Palestinian 'elections are now the only means through which the PA can regain popular legitimacy, Hamas can be integrated into the Palestinian political system and Fatah can be united behind a single political will'.[14] The alternative to elections is almost certainly political and institutional collapse. Very simply, given the depth of the crisis in the Palestinian leadership, the struggle for internal Palestinian democracy can no longer be postponed and seen as a consequence of independence: it has become a precondition.

Another is how the Palestinians can build on the enormous diplomatic victory provided by the advisory opinion of the International Court of Justice (ICJ), 'the most important development in the Palestinian cause since 1967', in the opinion of PA Foreign Minister Nasser El Kidwa, who, as Palestinian representative to the United Nations, did much to bring it about.

The ICJ opinion went beyond simply confirming the legality and justice of the Palestinians' case – that the wall and the settlements it defends (including those in East Jerusalem) are illegal under every tenet of international law and must be dismantled with reparation for their victims. It also ruled that Israel's right to security could not be invoked to deny the Palestinians' right to self-determination. On the contrary, it unequivocally ruled that these 'rights and obligations are a matter of law and not negotiations, that Palestinians have legal rights not subject to negotiations nor derived from them', says Vaughan Lowe, public international law expert and member of the Palestinian delegation to ICJ proceedings at The Hague.[15]

The ICJ also provides the necessary corpus of law to mount a campaign for the enforcement of the opinion first at the United Nations and then, should this fail, through strategies for boycotts, divestments and sanctions by civic organizations, public bodies and ultimately states. To argue that such a campaign will be victim to the US veto at the UN Security Council is to miss the point. The point is to isolate Israel and the United States in the court of international legal and public opinion. And there is no higher body in that court than the ICJ, no body that is more difficult for law-based states to ignore.

The final challenge is for Palestinians to decide their attitude to Israeli opinion, and especially the peace movement, arguably their most important potential ally in the struggle against occupation. The rural campaigns against the wall have brought Palestinian and Israeli peace activists together as no other since the second *intifada* erupted in 2000 and consigned the two peoples to their respective ghettos: ideological in the case of the Israelis and physical in the case of the Palestinians.

The ICJ ruling has also provided new bases for that partnership, one based on a genuinely anti-colonial practice and discourse. As Kimmerling has argued, the greatest failures of the Israeli left in the second *intifada* have been not to support the officers refusing to serve in the occupied territories, not to prosecute the Israeli state for war crimes, not to back international campaigns for sanctions and boycotts, and not to obey the moral 'imperative which unequivocally states that occupying and subjugating a people, unnecessarily colonising them, and robbing them of their land and water are profound sins'.[16]

The greatest failure of the Palestinian left, as Bishara has argued, has been to refuse to point out to their Israeli counterparts that their 'current slogan of separation is actually a racist slogan; it legitimises Israel's ongoing domination of another people; it legitimises the idea that the Palestinians are a demographic threat. In its stead we must propagate a politics that emphasises binational values of equality, reciprocity and coexistence.'[17]

The assumption of Kimmerling and Bishara – modelled on precedents like Vietnam and South Africa – is that no anti-colonial movement can ultimately succeed without causing a fracture in the people of the colonial power. That fracture is possible. Thirty-eight years after their conquest there is still no Israeli consensus over the fate of the occupied territories, as the fissures caused by the Gaza disengagement attest. They remain Israel's weakest, most contested, most vulnerable possession.

CONCLUSION

Eqbal Ahmad wrote in 1984 that one of the many ironies of history was that Israel's first, successful colonisation of Palestine occurred at the very moment when de-colonisation struggles in India, Burma, Ceylon and China were reaching victory.[18] For years Palestinians believed their fate would be similarly resolved, either through Arab recovery or through the inspiring

[29]

examples subsequently blazed by Algeria, Vietnam and South Africa.

Residues of those hopes remain in the Palestinian national movement today. Among the PA leadership there is still the visceral belief that the occupation of the West Bank and Gaza will somehow retreat due to its very illegality and its historical injustice. The Islamists too, for all their activism, have the same passive belief in a restorative destiny: that all the Palestinians really need to do is hold fast to Jerusalem and the right of return and wait for the Arab world to recover its faith, and then Israel somehow will collapse, if not by war, then through demography or through what in their eyes is the fundamental contradiction of being a Jewish state in an Arab Islamic milieu.

Neither scenario is especially likely. For what Ahmad also pointed out was that Israeli colonialism bore scant resemblance to that which ruled India, Algeria, Vietnam or even South Africa. For all its modern origins Zionism harked back to more classic forms of settler colonialism, providing a haven and a power, 'an iron wall' to protect its people. Unlike the later regimes, its primary purpose was not to exploit the native population, even if exploitation did occur. It was rather to exclude the indigenous population as a national and political force.

At the time of its establishment Israel successfully implemented this exclusionary policy, largely through the enormous act of ethnic cleansing that was deliberately wrought through the 1948 war. It has been less successful with the 1967 conquests. The fact of Palestinian resistance has forced on Israel some sort of territorial and demographic compromise, and expedited wholly new forms of neo-colonial control and containment, whose purpose was best described by the Israeli writer Amira Hass as demographic 'separation of the two peoples with the appearance of political separation but with only one government – Israel – having the power to effect the destinies of both'.[19] The dual policy represents what can only be called the peculiar, paranoid strain in Israeli colonialism. Due to the existential fears out of which the Jewish state was born – and through which it sustains its legitimacy, especially among its actual and potential Jewish citizenry – it seeks always to be rid of the Palestinians. But out of precisely the same fears, it seeks always to control them.

That control is realised through Israel's system of rule in the occupied territories, with the wall being its most lethal, potentially most irreversible, component. Such a system cannot be removed by the passive resistance offered by diplomacy, or by uncoordinated, vengeful armed resistance. It has to be outflanked, dismantled, out-administered, out-argued and rendered inoperative through strategies that are 'historically rooted, tactically flexible, diplomatically consistent and politically virtuoso', in Eqbal Ahmad's words,[20] a political war of position that is also a popular war of manoeuvre. The third strategy described above marks a step in that direction. It may prove no more successful than the other two. But it is the only road left to Palestine or what is left of Palestine. And it must begin by tearing down Israel's latest, most brutal, most outrageous and most audacious form of exclusion and control: the West Bank wall.

NOTES

1. See David Hirst, *The Gun and the Olive Branch: The Roots of Violence in the Middle East* (Faber and Faber, revised edition, 2003).
2. Baruch Kimmerling, *Politicide: Ariel Sharon's War Against the Palestinians* (Verso, 2003).
3. Graham Usher, 'Bantustanisation or binationalism?' in *Dispatches from Palestine: The Rise and Fall of the Oslo Peace Process* (Pluto Press, 1999).

4. Graham Usher, 'Closures, cantons and the Palestinian Covenant', in *Dispatches from Palestine*.

5. See Avi Shlaim, *The Iron Wall: Israel and the Arab World* (Penguin, 2000).

6. Ari Shavit, 'The big freeze', *Ha'aretz*, 8 October 2004.

7. Quoted in Aluf Benn, 'Israel's identity crisis', *Salonweb*, 16 May 2005. <http://www.salon.com/news/feature/2005/05/16/identity/index.html> (accessed on 21 October 2005).

8. Ibid.

9. Ibid.

10. Interview with author, August 2001.

11. For an account of the 'revised' Jordan option, see Gary Sussman, 'Ariel Sharon and the Jordan option', MERIP online report, March 2005. <http://www.merip.org/mero/interventions/sussman_interv.html> (accessed on 21 October 2005).

12. Interview with author, February 2005.

13. Interview with author, June 2000.

14. Interview with author, May 2004.

15. Speech delivered in Ramallah on first anniversary of ICJ advisory opinion. <http://www.palestine-pmc.com/details.asp?cat=4&id=2030> (accessed on 13 October 2005).

16. Baruch Kimmerling, *Politicide*.

17. Interview with author, August 2001.

18. Eqbal Ahmad, 'Pioneering in the nuclear age: an essay on Israel and the Palestinians', *Race & Class*, spring 1984.

19. Amira Hass, 'Israel's closure policy: an ineffective strategy of containment and repression', *Journal of Palestine Studies*, spring 2002.

20. Eqbal Ahmad, 'Pioneering in the nuclear age'.

Constructing the wall at Hizma, West Bank

1 Wall and Route

'BEAUTIFUL PHOTOS'

On 29 July 2003, Israeli Prime Minister Ariel Sharon and US President George W. Bush met at the White House. Sharon was the foreign leader most favoured in Washington: it was his eighth visit to the White House and his tenth official meeting with the president. The Bush administration was sympathetic to Sharon's right-wing Likud Party to a degree unusual even by partisan US standards, and this regard had increased after '9/11' and Sharon's efforts to portray his counter-insurgency measures in the West Bank and Gaza Strip as part of the global war against terrorism. Sharon, therefore, had every reason to expect a cordial reception from his host, and yet a certain disquiet preceded his meeting.

Four days earlier at the same venue, Bush had hosted the new Palestinian prime minister, Abu Mazen. The Bush administration hoped that Abu Mazen would use his newly created position to wrest power from the Palestinian Authority's President Yasser Arafat, who was discredited in US eyes as an obstacle to peace. Abu Mazen was also crucial to the success of the Road Map, the recently launched peace initiative. Bush was thus uncharacteristically attentive to Palestinian concerns. At their meeting Abu Mazen raised the issue of the wall. His concern was somewhat belated as the first phase of construction, some 125 kilometres through the northern West Bank, was due for completion in less than a week. Local farmers, human rights organisations and international solidarity groups had been warning of the wall's negative political and humanitarian impact since the first olive tree had been felled almost a year earlier. The Palestinian Authority had been laggard in its response, but grassroots pressure was such that Abu Mazen could not afford to ignore the issue if he was to maintain credibility with the Palestinian public.

Abu Mazen expressed the hope that Bush would demand a complete halt to construction of the wall. At the very least, he urged, the president should use his influence to have the wall re-routed towards the 'Green Line' – the internationally recognised border between Israel and the West Bank – and stem its intrusion into Palestinian territory. The president listened attentively and appeared to take Abu Mazen's considerations on board, especially his account of the suffering the wall was inflicting on ordinary Palestinians. At their joint press conference afterwards, Bush described the wall as 'a problem', declaring that it was 'very difficult to develop confidence between the Palestinians and Israel with a wall snaking through the West Bank'.

Such publicly expressed reservations were unwelcome to Sharon, as was Bush's referring to the 'wall' with its connotations of a permanent border: Israel preferred the more homely term 'fence'. Before his encounter with Bush, Sharon had scheduled a separate meeting with National Security Advisor Condoleeza Rice at which he requested that the president stop using the expression 'wall'. Rice explained that Bush used the terms 'fence' and 'wall' interchangeably and that no political inference should be drawn. At this point, Sharon reached for his photos:

> beautiful photos, as members of his entourage put it, of the fence being built, which prove that it is not a wall,

but rather a barrier comprised of fences and patrol routes . . . [produced] to offset the impression of the presentation that the Palestinians brought on the same issue – trying to show that it is a wall.[1]

In his meeting with Bush the following day, 'the best and most intimate meeting to date', Sharon's concerns were put to rest. '"Ariel", Bush kept referring to Sharon, and underscored his points by touching the Prime Minister's knee often.' Bush brought up the subject of the wall and its impact on the Palestinian population. 'This issue troubles us because we are aware of the price that the rural population is paying. People are being cut off from their fields. Something has to be done about that.' Sharon pulled out a photographed copy of Robert Frost's poem, *Mending Wall* and presented it to Bush. He quoted the last line, 'Good fences make good neighbours'. 'Construction on the fence will continue', he declared, 'but I promise to check how damage to the daily life of the Palestinian population can be reduced.'[2]

At their joint press conference afterwards, Sharon praised Bush as a world leader in the fight against terrorism and vowed that Israel, like the United States, would never surrender to terror and evil. For his part, Bush referred to the 'fence' rather than the 'wall', which was downgraded from a 'problem' to a 'sensitive issue'. Following the Washington meetings, construction of the wall was not halted or reversed as Abu Mazen had requested, and as the UN General Assembly and the International Court of Justice (ICJ) would later demand. Five weeks later, Abu Mazen resigned as Palestinian prime minister, undermined both by Sharon and by Arafat who had their different reasons for wanting his downfall. However, he would be back at the White House in May 2005, this time as Palestinian Authority President, successor to the deceased Arafat. Again, the wall would be one of the main issues raised, but by then it had become another Israeli 'fact on the ground', snaking through the West Bank with an air of permanency, with the Palestinian rural population – now trapped in enclaves and 'closed areas' – still paying the price.

WALL OR FENCE?

What are the components of the structure that Sharon's 'beautiful photos' portrayed as nothing more substantial than a fence? According to the official Ministry of Defence website, the fence is only one element of 'a multilayered composite obstacle'.[3] This is a wire-and-mesh 'intrusion-detection' or 'smart' fence, approximately three metres high, mounted on a concrete base. It is equipped with electronic sensors, including cameras with night vision capacity, to warn of infiltration attempts. An intruder touching the fence triggers a signal to a nearby command centre or 'war room' where military personnel monitor computers and television screens. As each section of the route is numbered, a military unit can be deployed to the affected locale within eight minutes.[4]

The 'smart' fence is augmented by a number of static security features. On at least one and usually both sides of the fence are paved roads for patrol vehicles. Smoothed strips of sand on either side of the patrol road will show the footprints of any intruders. On the 'Palestinian side' there is a ditch or trench 'or other means intended to prevent motor vehicles from crashing into and through the fence'. This is flanked by a pyramid-shaped stack of coiled razor wire, some two metres tall. An additional razor wire barrier lies on the 'Israeli side'. The complete obstacle is generally between 30 and 70 metres wide, although it spans 100 metres in certain areas. Signs are placed on the razor wire on the Palestinian side with warnings in Arabic, Hebrew and English which read: 'Mortal danger: military zone. Any person who passes or damages the fence endangers his life.'

The major part of the barrier is composed of this multi-layered system. The remainder is made up of precast concrete sections, generally eight metres high. According to the Israeli authorities, these concrete sections are built 'in areas where the threat of sniper fire is real and immediate or in areas where it was impossible to build a fence for topographical reasons.'[5] In practice, such sections are erected alongside Palestinian population centres close to the Green Line, such as the towns of Qalqilya and Tulkarm, where the wall is capped with surveillance towers and cameras. Concrete slabs also dominate much of the 'Jerusalem Envelope', the term employed by the Israeli authorities for the wall around the greater Jerusalem area, including large sections of the adjoining Ramallah and Bethlehem districts. The concrete wall appears more formidable and oppressive, especially as it predominates in built-up urban areas. It should be borne in mind, however, that the more extensive 'fence' segment takes up more Palestinian land for its 'footprint' than the wall segments, and that it is equally effective – and destructive – in terms of its security and humanitarian impact.

It is disingenuous to describe such a formidable construction as a 'fence', a term which cannot convey the magnitude of a structure that carves a 670-kilometre path through the West Bank landscape. The undertaking is the largest infrastructure project in Israel's history: as one Israeli commentator observed, 'even the national water carrier or the draining of the Hula swamps look like an exercise in sandcastles compared to this colossal project'.[6] Nor does it appear temporary, for all the Israeli claims to the contrary: as the same commentator

---

Buffer zones

Some military personnel have recommended the creation of a buffer zone along the West Bank wall similar to the one in the Gaza Strip. The chief advocate of this measure is Major-General Doron Almog, who was responsible for rebuilding the fence around the Gaza Strip, following its partial demolition by Palestinians at the start of the second *intifada*. According to Almog, 'a comprehensive defensive model is needed to help compensate for these potential failures in the [West Bank] fence itself'. What is lacking specifically are 'bulldozed security buffer zones and special rules of engagement for those military personnel responsible for monitoring the fence and its environs.'[7] In the Gaza Strip, the bulldozed buffer zone is one kilometre wide, and trees and vegetation have been uprooted to allow the Israeli military an unobstructed view of the terrain. The standard rules of engagement have also been eased so that any Palestinian entering this zone is assumed to have aggressive intentions and can be shot. The first indication of the adoption of a buffer zone in the West Bank came in November 2004 when Palestinian officials were informed that new military orders prohibit new construction within a distance of 300 metres on the Palestinian side of the wall in the Qalqilya and Tulkarm districts.

---

observed, 'You have to be almost insane to think that somebody uprooted mountains, levelled hills and poured billions here in order to build some temporary security barrier "until the permanent borders are decided".' Its permanent nature is borne out by the cost, which doubled from an initial estimate of 8 million shekels ($US 1.75 million) per kilometre when the project started in 2002 to 15 million shekels per kilometre by February

2004.[8] Sums of between \$US1 and 3.4 billion have been cited for the overall cost. By 2005, the estimate was 5.6 billion shekels (\$US 1.3 billion)[9] and the high cost of construction was cited by the State of Israel in the High Court as a reason not to alter the route, 'as it would be very expensive to move'.[10] Although the term 'barrier' is often employed to describe the structure, this implies that the main purpose is the stated one of providing a security obstacle to prevent the infiltration of Palestinians into Israel. While accepting that it also fulfils this function, 'wall' more accurately conveys its true purpose, even if most of the structure does not constitute a wall in the strict sense of the word. However, as the International Court of Justice observed, the term wall 'cannot be understood in a limited physical sense,'[11] and the term 'wall' best conveys the main purpose and significance of the project, which is to obliterate the internationally-recognised Green Line and to create a new border deeper within West Bank territory, in the process annexing major settlements, territory and water resources to Israel.

BORDERS AND BARRIERS

Reflecting its conflict-ridden history – and its refusal to declare where its official borders lie – demarcation lines and defensive barriers have marked Israel's boundaries with its neighbours. The best known of these is the 1949 'armistice demarcation line' or 'Green Line', separating Israel from the then Jordanian-ruled West Bank and East Jerusalem. The Green Line ceased to exist after Israel's occupation of the West Bank in 1967, although it remains the internationally recognised border as far as the international community is concerned. The boundary with the Gaza Strip also disappeared in 1967: a fence was constructed along Gaza's relatively short borders with Israel following the Israeli military withdrawal from the Strip in the mid-1990s, and rebuilt and strengthened during the second *intifada*.[12] Barriers to prevent infiltrations have also been constructed by Israel along its border with Lebanon, along the occupied Syrian Golan Heights and in the Jordan Valley.

Israel's policy since 1967 of colonising the West Bank through Jewish settlement and of attracting Palestinian day labourers into Israel militated against a reinstatement of a physical barrier along the old Green Line. The porous boundary between Israel and the West Bank survived the first *intifada* of the late 1980s, the suicide bombings in Israeli cities of the mid-1990s and the years of the Oslo Accords, although the number of Palestinian labourers commuting daily into Israel dropped sharply due to the imposition of a 'closure policy', which severely restricted Palestinian internal and external movement. This changed with the devastating wave of West Bank-originated suicide attacks in the second *intifada*. The apparent effectiveness of the Gaza fence in preventing suicide bombers from the Gaza Strip from infiltrating into Israel led to demands from the Israeli public for a similar structure along the West Bank.

However, the differences between the two remnants of historic Palestine are considerable. The Gaza Strip has the Mediterranean Sea to its west and a fortified border with Egypt to the south, which from the time of the Israeli-Egyptian peace treaty of 1982 until the second *intifada* had remained largely quiet. The section of the Strip abutting Israel proper is 50 kilometres in length, compared to the 315-kilometre Green Line. Gaza's relatively flat and sandy topography ensured that construction of a barrier was technically undemanding and inexpensive. Furthermore, the Gaza barrier does not separate Palestinians from their lands or from one another, although it confines over a million inhabitants to one of world's smallest and most densely populated territories. The Gaza barrier was also built on the original demarcation line, so that Israel's right to build a structure on internationally recognised borders has not been legally challenged. By contrast, the Green Line winds much further through more difficult terrain. In 1967 Israel also conquered and later illegally annexed Arab East Jerusalem, investing the city with the status of its 'eternal and undivided capital'. The insertion of Jewish settlements throughout East Jerusalem and its environs makes a separation of the Arab and Jewish populations there virtually impossible.

Despite such technical difficulties, plans to cordon off all or parts of the West Bank and to block the unregulated entry of Palestinians into Israel go back to the mid-1990s, and took on greater urgency with the outbreak of the second *intifada*. In November 2000, Prime Minister Ehud Barak approved a plan to establish a barrier along a section of the northern and central West Bank to prevent vehicles crossing into Israel. This was not initially implemented, and an estimated 70,000 day labourers continued to commute to their jobs across the Green Line as late as February 2002, at the same time as a regime of checkpoints, earth mounds and trenches was crippling social and economic life within the West Bank itself.

With a rising civilian toll from suicide bombs inside Israel, the new Prime Minister Ariel Sharon bowed to public pressure. In June 2001, he established a steering committee, under National Security Council director Uzi Dayan, to come up with a more comprehensive plan to prevent Palestinians from infiltrating into Israel. The steering committee's recommendations led to the implementation of Barak's earlier plan and suggestions of a pedestrian barrier along certain high-risk locations along the 'seam zone' – a strip of land extending on both sides of the Green Line. It was not until April 2002, however, after an especially lethal round of suicide attacks inside Israeli cities, that the Israeli cabinet approved a decision to establish a pedestrian barrier in three areas of the West Bank. A Seam Zone Administration was established and the Israeli Defence Forces (IDF) began requisitioning and levelling land. By June 2002 the Seam Zone Administration had formulated a plan to build Phase I of the wall, through the northern part of the West Bank and parts of the 'Jerusalem Envelope'. The plan was approved in principle by the cabinet in Government Decision 2077 in June 2002, and formally approved in August.[13]

Secrecy characterised the route from the beginning. The Israeli human rights organisation B'Tselem requested a map of the route from the Ministry of Defence but was informed that publication was not authorised, a policy 'that flagrantly violates the rules of proper administration and hampers informed public debate on a project of long-term, far-reaching significance'.[14] The government did not publish an official map of the complete route until October 2003 and maps of the ongoing phases were based on land levelling, progress in construction and local maps distributed by the IDF as part of the land requisitioning process. According to the cabinet-approved plan of February 2005, the wall will extend some 670 kilometres with just 20 per cent running along the Green Line, with the rest located inside the West Bank (apart from a few kilometres inside Israel proper).[15] No target date was set for completion, and the much-delayed project was not expected to be finished before the middle of 2006.[16]

The wall was not constructed in one continuous segue but in different phases. Phase I, through the Jenin, Tulkarm and Qalqilya districts in the northern West Bank, was officially completed in July 2003 (Chapter 2 examines the impact of this phase on the local Palestinian population). In January 2003, work began on Phase II, a 45-kilometre-long section running east into the Jordan Valley which, combined with Phase I, completely seals off the northern West Bank. The long route through the central and southern sections of the West Bank, Phase III, was initially approved in October 2003. Intruding deep into the West Bank to encircle Ariel and surrounding settlements, this proved to be the most controversial phase and led to protracted negotiations with the US administration before the route was finally approved in February 2005 (see Chapter 4). The 'Jerusalem Envelope' encircling the Jerusalem area and parts of the Ramallah and Bethlehem districts also results in major disruption to Palestinian life; because of its importance as a political, social, economic, religious and cultural centre for Palestinians, the Jerusalem wall is examined in Chapter 3.

DETERMINING THE ROUTE

That Israeli citizens face a severe security threat is beyond dispute. Since the second *intifada* erupted in late 2000, over 400 Israeli fatalities and many more injuries have been caused by Palestinian suicide bombers. Most of these attacks have taken place on buses or in shopping malls, restaurants and hotels, and the majority of those killed and maimed have been civilians, including women and children. The militants' claims that they are retaliating for the greater number of Palestinian civilians killed or that suicide bombings are a legitimate response to Israel's superior weaponry in no way justify such attacks, which have been condemned by human rights groups as crimes against humanity.[17]

The vast majority of suicide attacks have been perpetrated by militants from the West Bank, testifying to the efficacy of the Gaza barrier in thwarting infiltrations into Israel. Since completion of the wall in the northern West Bank, attacks from former militant strongholds such as the cities of Tulkarm and Jenin have virtually ceased, with evidence that militants are diverting their attention to the south and middle of Israel where the wall is not yet built.[18] Israeli sources cite an 80 per cent drop in suicide attacks in the first six months of 2004 compared with the same period the previous year.[19] However, this decline is also attributable to better intelligence, an escalated policy of assassination of militants and Israel's reoccupation of the major West Bank cities.

Israel has the right 'and indeed the duty, to respond in order to protect the life of its citizens' as the ICJ noted in its advisory opinion, but '[t]he measures taken are bound nonetheless to remain in conformity with applicable international law'.[20] Given that the violation of international law occurs because of the wall's intrusion into the West Bank and East Jerusalem, would the wall have been any less effective – for its stated purpose of thwarting suicide bombers – had it been built along the internationally-recognised Green Line? As Noam Chomsky observes, a Green Line wall could 'be as forbidding as the authorities chose: patrolled by the army on both sides, heavily mined, impenetrable. Such a wall would maximize security, and there would be no international protest or violation of international law.'[21] A Green Line wall would have been completed in a much shorter time and at half the cost of the current 670-kilometre structure.[22] It would also require fewer troops to monitor and patrol, would not corral Palestinian villages into enclaves and closed areas and would thus dispense with the need for a discriminatory gate and permit regime.

In fact, the 45-kilometre Phase II section in the northern Jenin area is built close to the Green Line, although still constructed within the West Bank. Since its completion no suicide bomber has succeeded in breaching this section to perpetrate an attack inside Israel. Phase II does not isolate Palestinian communities within closed areas nor has it led to major humanitarian problems. A survey led by the World Bank found that 'the prospect of physical separation and isolation in northern Jenin governorate, with inhabitants effectively cut off from workplaces, agricultural lands, irrigation networks, water resources, and/or school, health clinics and other social services, is much less than the affected areas near Tulkarm and Qalqilya of Phase 1'.[23]

Given the effectiveness of the Phase II section from the point of view of security, and its minimal humanitarian impact, why was the wall in its entirety not built along the Green Line? This would have prevented international criticism, the UN resolutions and the referral of the question to the International Court of Justice, where the issue was not Israel's right to build a wall per se, but the legal consequence of the route through the West Bank and East Jerusalem. Israeli officials insist that the route was determined solely by security, operational and topographic considerations, and deny that its path through the West Bank is a pretext to unilaterally establish a new border and annex Palestinian land. The State of Israel set out the principal considerations that determined the route in its response to a High Court petition, the *Al-Hadi* case. The first was topographic: 'The barrier must pass through, to the greatest extent possible, areas from which the surrounding territory can be controlled, in order to prevent harm to forces operating along the route, and to enable the forces to operate observation points that overlook both sides of the fence'.[24]

The security benefits of locating the wall on higher ground are self-evident. However, such strategic heights are not always located on the Palestinian side of the Green Line, through which 80 per cent of the route runs. A wall with significant segments built inside Israel, rather than a negligible few kilometres, would have demonstrated that the objective is security rather than an annexation of Palestinian territory. Instead, a tour of the Qalqilya and Tulkarm areas leads to the suspicion that the planners eschewed higher ground if constructing the wall on lower terrain meant more Palestinian land would fall on the Israeli side. B'Tselem notes that a particular section of the route 'runs along a dry river bed at the foot of Jayous', isolating most of the village's land on the Israeli side of the wall: 'In other words not only is the route in this area based on illegitimate considerations, it is even contrary to military needs, which dictate that the route run along high areas to the greatest extent possible.'[25]

A second argument for locating the wall some distance inside the West Bank was set out in response to the same petition. 'The fear is that the barrier will not prevent every penetration, and that security forces will not be able to arrive in time to thwart the crossing of potential attackers. A geographic security area is necessary to enable the combat forces to chase the terrorists within Judea and Samaria [the West Bank] before they are able to cross into Israel and disappear within the population'.[26]

This argument that additional 'warning space' is needed to apprehend intruders who succeed in penetrating the wall's defences also appears reasonable from a security point of view. However, as Chomsky points out, the money saved on a less expensive and shorter route along the Green Line could have been employed to build a more secure and impenetrable barrier. Moreover, members of the Council for Peace and Security, a group of high-ranking ex-military and intelligence personnel, disagree that defensive depth necessarily provides the best security: 'Once the terrorist has found a way over the fence, he moves in less than a minute over 14 metres or 30 metres. Security is provided by the type of fence, because that is where the terrorist can be caught.'[27]

A wide security area also brings the wall closer to Palestinian houses where 'it will be easier to sabotage the fence and target soldiers on patrol. . . . Any child playing ball near the fence could activate the alarm system and cause a needless military alert.'[28] An extended security area also results in greater numbers of Palestinians being cut off from their land and services and a corresponding need for crossing points, thus 'creating friction and the kind of security threat that the fence itself is meant to eliminate or reduce'.[29] Frustration is also increased by the threat to the livelihood and viability of rural communities: 'Making it harder for the residents to earn a living will only increase their bitterness and anger. . . . That in itself creates a serious threat to Israeli security.'[30] In any case, the 'warning space' argument is further undermined by the fact that in many cases such land is actually intended to provide the future expansion of settlements. As B'Tselem points out, 'the designation of certain land for residential use, on the one hand, and "warning space" on the other hand, [is] mutually exclusive. You cannot achieve both.'[31]

Although the issue of Jewish settlements located inside the West Bank is not mentioned in official Israeli arguments for the wall, in its response to the *Al-Hadi* case, the state named the protection of these settlements as a third reason for determining the route. 'The fear is that erection of the barrier will channel the attacks to these communities, so it was decided to have the fence pass east of these settlements in order to provide protection for them and for the access roads that reach them.'[32] Given that the settlements have been established contrary to international law, the requisitioning of additional land to protect them represents a further violation: 'In effect, Palestinians are being told that Israel must steal more Palestinian land to protect Israelis living on previously stolen Palestinian land.'[33] A solution would be to disband the settlements entirely and move the settlers into Israel proper. Alternatively, a main wall could have been built along the Green Line and barriers constructed around individual settlements. As B'Tselem observes: "The existence of these two alternatives, which Israel chose to ignore, raises concern that the real reason for the cabinet's decision on the barrier's route was not to provide maximum protection of the settlers . . . [but] to establish facts on the ground that would perpetuate the existence of settlements and facilitate their future annexation into Israel.'[34]

THE HIJACK: 'WE'VE MOVED THE GREEN LINE'

The final route of the wall, approved by the cabinet in February 2005, results from Israel's long-standing ambition to annex the major settlement blocs illegally constructed on West Bank territory. Hence the wall's circuitous route away from the Green Line and deep into the West Bank to encompass these blocs. Only in Phase II, where there are no settlement blocs to encompass, does the wall approximately follow the 1949 demarcation line. However, when plans for Phase I were drawn up in 2002 an annexationist route was not originally intended: the 'basic idea was to follow the Green Line', according to Binyamin Ben-Eliezer, the Defence Minister in the coalition government. Ben-Eliezer also confirms that before he left office his ministry had drawn up a plan for the remaining sections of the wall with a 'a general order to continue the route . . . as close as possible to the Green Line'.[35]

A wall along the Green Line was anathema to the settlers, however. They had spent years obliterating that boundary and had no desire to see a new border established – albeit one to the east of the old demarcation line – which would leave many settlements on the Palestinian side and signify an end to their dreams of a 'Greater Israel'. In June 2002, the head of YESHA, the Settlers' Council, warned that 'if a separation fence is erected, we will break up the [government] coalition'.[36] In their opposition to the wall the settlers had the support of Prime Minister Ariel Sharon, the main driving force behind decades of settlement expansion. According to Ben-Eliezer, Sharon 'would have preferred not to have built [a wall], because it broke a conception and created a situation in which *de facto* we were establishing a border'.[37] However, the settlers' objections went against the wishes of the Israeli public who wanted a wall built as quickly as possible – anywhere as long as it kept the suicide bombers out. Hence the 'hijack': 'Once Prime Minister Sharon and settlement leaders realized they could not withstand the public pressure, they reversed their previous fierce opposition to the fence and instead directed their efforts into changing the line of demarcation that was drawn up by the military . . . to include within the fence as many settlements as possible, in order to convey the message that Israel intended to annex them in any potential settlement of the conflict.'[38]

From this point on Sharon, with the assistance of influential settlers, was the prime mover in determining the route, 'keeping close tabs on the plan', visiting the site often and sketching where the route should run.[39] He was granted an unprecedented degree of freedom in determining the route: Government Decision 2077 stated that 'the precise and final route will be determined by the prime minister and the minister of defence'.[40] The settlers' first success was in changing the route in the already-approved Phase I so that the wall would encompass the settlement of Alfei Menashe, five kilometres east of the major Palestinian town of Qalqilya, which was to be left on the Palestinian side according to the initial plan. Eliezer Hasdai, head of the local council and member of the Likud Central Committee, intervened. 'According to the first plan . . . the fence was supposed to be close to the Green Line. I undertook a great deal of political activity, Sharon and Fuad [Minister of Defence Ben-Eliezer] came to visit me and agreed to put Alfei Menashe inside and to "wrap" the fence around it.'[41] As a result of this pressure, Qalqilya city was surrounded on all sides by the wall and five Palestinian villages bordering Alfei Menashe settlement found themselves isolated in a closed area and severed from the rest of the West Bank (see Chapter 2 and Map 2). 'We've gone very far from the original plan,' Hasdai boasted. 'We've moved the Green Line.'[42]

So far, apart from Alfei Menashe, the settlements enclosed by the wall were relatively small and close to the Green Line, although the inclusion of rich land and water resources for their future growth seriously threatened the survival of many Palestinian borderline communities (see Chapter 2). The real territorial gains would come in the centre and south of the West Bank, including Jerusalem, if a route could be devised to encompass the large 'settlement blocs', clusters of strategic and demographic importance. In early 2003, the settlers' YESHA Council proposed a route plan to secure these aims – 'maximum Jewish population, minimum Arab population and maximum territory' – which would bring dozens of settlements and more than 100,000 Palestinians to the Israeli side of the wall.[43] A key prize was Ariel, one of the largest West Bank settlements and a Likud stronghold, strategically located on a series of hills ranging 22 kilometres into the West Bank. Ariel was situated on the east–west Trans-Samaria highway which extends into the Jordan Valley, and its eastern edge was close to the principal north–south highway, Route 60. If combined with a rumoured 'Jordan Valley wall', it would drive a horizontal wedge between the northern and southern West Bank. What would become known as the 'Ariel Finger' included numerous other settlements, providing a large and contiguous expanse of territory as a buffer to the Tel Aviv metropolitan area, thickening Israel's 'waist' at one of its narrowest points (See Map 1).

The original, more security-oriented route drawn up by Ben-Eliezer did not include Ariel. The Mayor of Ariel, Ron Nahman, as powerful in Sharon's Likud party as Eliezer Hasdai, vehemently objected. 'I fought against this plan from the start. Fuad [Ben-Eliezer] and the Labor Party wanted to abandon us, to leave 50,000 Jews outside the fence.' Nahman had little success initially, but his luck turned with the replacement of Ben-Eliezer by the hawkish Shaul Mofaz as Defence Minister in Sharon's second-term government. 'In early May Mofaz told him festively that it was decided for good that Ariel would be inside the fence.'[44] However, while the first phases of construction in the northern West Bank were unfolding largely out of the public eye, Phase III was coming under greater scrutiny from the international community, because of the deeper intrusions into the West Bank and the impact on Jerusalem and Bethlehem. The Road Map was also finally showing signs of life with the arrival of Abu Mazen as Palestinian prime minister. 'Moving the Green Line' so radically as to include Ariel would now be more difficult, especially as the Road Map called for a halt to such attempts at geo-political engineering. Indeed, the Bush Administration balked at the massive appropriation of territory the Ariel Finger represented. For their part, settler representatives in the Knesset delayed budget allocations for a wall that didn't encompass the major settlement blocs.[45] Caught between these opposing pressures, most of 2003 passed without Sharon bringing the central and southern stages of the wall before the cabinet for approval, despite criticism that his delay was costing lives.

Sharon first had to receive the all-important US imprimatur, and in the 'breach plan' the two sides devised a compromise that satisfied both US concerns and Sharon's strategic objectives. Under the 'breach plan', individual barriers or 'fingernails' would be erected around the main Ariel bloc settlements,

A Jordan Valley wall?

Although the plan never appeared on official maps there were consistent reports throughout 2003 of an Israeli proposal to construct an additional wall along the Jordan Valley. The desert terrain supports few Palestinian population centres, apart from Jericho, while Israel has invested in sustained and costly settlement building along the entire length of the valley north of the Dead Sea. The wall would be made up of fences and ditches and follow the natural topography of mountain and clifftops, creating a buffer zone between the West Bank and Jordan.

Sharon was known to be keen on maintaining Israel's hold of the Jordan Valley which, like the major settlement blocs to the west, he believed essential for Israel's long term security.[46] Not surprisingly, the Jordan Valley wall featured prominently in Palestinian warnings of Sharon's strategy of dividing the Palestinian-populated parts of the West Bank into non-contiguous cantons surrounded by settlement blocs and security zones.

David Levy, the head of the Jordan Valley Council – the regional settlement administration – recounted that Sharon showed him a map of the route of the Jordan Valley wall. '[A]ccording to that map, the fence will keep all of the Jordan Valley and the Judean Desert under Israel's control, a 20–30 kilometre wide strip. Just as it appears in maps that Sharon has been showing for years. Such a fence, Levy says with satisfaction, is a political statement, a statement of annexing the Jordan Valley under cover of the "security fence."[47]

However, because of 'the likely negative political fallout in the international arena', the plan was dropped in the lead-up to the ICJ hearings.[48] A projected section in the northern Jordan valley that appeared in the first official map in October 2003 disappeared from the updated map that accompanied the Israeli cabinet's approval of the revised route of February 2005. However, according to the journalist Aluf Benn, Sharon still mentions the eastern wall 'to planners from time to time'.[49]

but these would not be linked together or connected to the main wall route for the moment. While the United States could claim to have delayed the most intrusive section of the wall, Sharon could also claim to have secured agreement that this bloc would be connected to the main wall in the future. Indeed, the first official map released in October 2003 showed all the settlements within the Ariel Finger encompassed by a single contiguous wall, which encompassed huge land reserves for future expansion. The United States also accepted the projected route in the Jerusalem, Ramallah and Bethlehem areas, which also delivered large settlements and their land reserves to the Israeli side of the wall. The only major settlement cluster left on the Palestinian side was the Maale Adumim bloc, located between East Jerusalem and Jericho. Its inclusion on the Israeli side at this stage would be politically problematic as it would sever East Jerusalem from the West Bank: a gap was left in the route at this critical point.

Having secured US agreement, and more than a year into construction, Sharon finally brought the route before the cabinet for approval, and it was passed by a large majority. Yossi Sarid of the left-wing Meretz party was unimpressed: 'This is a Swiss fence which has in more holes and breaches in it than security'. By contrast, the YESHA Council was jubilant: 'This is a victory for the security line'.[50] Dismayed by the Israeli cabinet decision, the PLO enlisted the intervention of the Arab League to bring the wall to the attention of the UN Security Council. Predictably, the United States, as a permanent member, vetoed a resolution condemning the wall as a violation of international law and calling for a halt to its construction. The Arab League next convened an emergency session of the General Assembly, where the United States had no veto power, at which the same resolution was passed unanimously, with strong EU support. Spurning international censure, Sharon vowed to press ahead with construction. Another emergency session of the Assembly was convened where, against the wishes of the United States and European Union, another resolution was passed, referring the question of the legality of the route to the International Court of Justice for a ruling.

This was a setback for Sharon. He believed that he had resolved the issue bilaterally to the satisfaction of the United States, but the Palestinians had succeeded in internationalising the question. Politically, the cabinet-approved route and official map showing the clear annexationist aims of the wall would be difficult to defend before the international community. On the humanitarian front he was also vulnerable, for the completed Phase I segment in the northern West Bank cut off rural communities from their land and essential services, with access dependent on the vagaries of the new gate and permit regime. Most difficult to justify was the plight of the villages trapped between the wall and the Green Line in the newly established closed areas. Why did a wall intended to protect Israelis from suicide bombers leave so many Palestinians on the Israeli side, with no physical obstacle between them and Israel proper?

Fearing that the route was indefensible on security grounds and that Israel would become the 'South Africa of today', Justice Minister Yosef Lapid proposed shortening the overall length by 200 kilometres. His proposal was rejected, as were three similar proposals submitted by opposition members of the Knesset. However, Sharon was himself moving to alter the route, not so radically as to give up on what he considered to be key strategic gains, but through tactical, 'humanitarian' adjustments. Throughout February 2004, in the lead-up to the ICJ deliberations, steps were taken to address the situation: a team was appointed to deal with humanitarian issues arising from the wall, millions of shekels were added to the defence budget for the construction of alternative roads and tunnels, and buses were provided for affected schoolchildren. There were reports that the plan to enclose clusters of Palestinian villages within double barriers would be cancelled and that large indents such as the Ariel Finger would be postponed indefinitely. Plans to build a wall along the Jordan valley were also quietly dropped. On the first day of the ICJ hearings, the IDF dismantled an 8-kilometre section of the wall from around the Palestinian town of Baqa Sharqiya, at one stroke removing the largest of the Palestinian enclaves and demonstrating the 'temporary' nature of the structure.

The International Court of Justice delivered its advisory opinion in July 2004. Having reviewed the written evidence and heard oral submissions the Court rejected Israel's contention 'that the specific course Israel has chosen for the wall was necessary to attain its security objectives'. Instead, the Court decided that 'the wall's sinuous route has been traced in such a way as to include . . . the great majority of the Israeli settlements in the occupied Palestinian Territory (including East Jerusalem)'. The Court ruled that where the route deviated into the West Bank and East Jerusalem, which was for most of its length, the wall violated international law and must be dismantled.[51] Predictably, Sharon rejected the ICJ opinion and pledged to continue construction. More difficult to ignore was a verdict that the Israeli High Court of Justice delivered a week before concerning the planned route of the wall near Beit Sourik in the Ramallah area. Declaring that there must be a proper balance between security and humanitarian considerations, the High Court ruled that the state had to alter 30 kilometres of the proposed route because of the disproportionate harm to local residents. While rejecting the ICJ ruling, Sharon acceded to the High Court decision which, crucially, had accepted the state's argument that the route was determined by security rather than political considerations and could be built in the West Bank. He ordered that the projected route should be revised in light of the principle of proportionality: however, neither the completed phases nor the 'Jerusalem Envelope' would be included in the revision.

In early 2004, Sharon announced his unilateral disengagement plan. In return for evacuating 21 settlements in the Gaza Strip and four inconsequential settlements in the West Bank, he vowed to maintain a secure hold of what he declared to be 'inseparable parts' of the West Bank, the main settlement blocs. In April 2004 he received official US endorsement for this objective in the form of a letter from President Bush informing him that 'new realities on the ground, including already existing major Israeli population centres', would have to be taken into consideration during final status negotiations.[52] The role of the wall in drawing the new frontier around the 'already existing major Israeli population centres' was clear. However, a revision of the cabinet-approved route of October 2003 was necessary, in light of alterations made in the lead-up to the ICJ hearings and new guidelines arising from the High Court case. Earlier plans to construct double barriers that would have isolated large numbers of Palestinian villages in the Salfit and Ramallah districts were dropped, as were plans to fence in seven communities and their 20,000 inhabitants in the Bethlehem district. It was also decided not to introduce closed areas or permits in the Bethlehem area because of criticism of the system in the northern West Bank. The most significant change to the route itself was in the southern Hebron area where the wall was brought significantly closer to the Green Line, a difficult decision for Sharon as land he coveted reverted to the Palestinian side.[53] However, the strategic settlement blocs remained on the Israeli side with individual barriers to be built around the main settlements in the Ariel Finger, which would be linked to the main wall in the future, as already agreed with the United States in the 'breach plan'.

Moreover, the new route brought one important addition to the Israeli side: Maale Adumim, the largest settlement in the West Bank. Strategically situated between Jerusalem and Jericho, Maale Adumim and its surrounding settlements had not been included in the previous cabinet-approved route because of expected US disapproval. As with Ariel settlement to the north, the route around Maale Adumim would serve as a 'contiguity breaker' between the central and southern West Bank, while also sealing off Palestinian East Jerusalem. Although the planners' revised proposal incorporating these changes was approved by Sharon and Mofaz in September 2004, Sharon waited until early 2005 before bringing the revised route before the cabinet for approval. He was prepared to trade off isolated settlements for the strategic goal of annexing the settlement blocs, but feared that the route modifications back towards the Green Line would be used as 'ammunition' by Jewish settlers enraged at his Gaza disengagement initiative. On the other hand, there would be international disapproval of the inclusion of Maale Adumim within the new officially approved route of the wall. The solution was to wait and bring both the disengagement plan and the revised route for approval at the same cabinet session in February 2005, again leading to complaints that his delay in completing the wall was costing lives.

THE NEW FRONTIER

The final route of the wall, therefore, is that approved by a large majority of the Israeli cabinet in February 2005. A major difference between this route and the first official plan approved in October 2003 is the decrease in the amount of land between the wall and the Green Line, down from more than 16 per cent to approximately 10 per cent of Palestinian territory. The other important distinction is the reduction in the number of Palestinians trapped between the wall and the Green Line, from an estimated 189,000 to 49,000. (This does not include over 200,000 Palestinians enclosed by the wall in the Jerusalem Envelope area who, as residents of Israel, are not subject to the same movement restrictions as West Bank Palestinians; see Chapter 3). The 2003 route, by consigning so many Palestinians to the Israeli side of a physical obstacle supposedly designed to prevent their unregulated entry into Israel, undermined the whole security rationale for the wall. That these numbers were reduced was not due to a prioritisation of the security argument but rather to international criticism – particularly in the run-up to the ICJ proceedings – and the belated intervention of the Israeli High Court (see Chapter 4). Despite the reduction in numbers, these 49,000 Palestinians are chief among those whose human rights are being violated by impediments to their liberty of movement and their rights to work, health, education and an adequate standard of living, as underlined in the ICJ advisory opinion. It also goes without saying that Israel has no authority under international law to unilaterally annex 10 per cent of Palestinian territory (with the connivance of the Bush administration).

In terms of territorial assets, the 10 per cent of land annexed represents major achievements for Sharon. Some 56 settlements containing approximately 170,000 settlers – 76 per cent of the West Bank settlement population – fall on the Israeli side of the wall, as do all the settlements in East Jerusalem. The major settlement blocs are included, the 'already existing major Israeli population centers' which the Bush letter agreed would accrue to Israel following the conclusion of peace negotiations. Moreover, the wall takes in not just the current boundaries of these settlements, but the huge reserves of land included in their master plans, guaranteeing the potential for massive growth in the future. In the meantime, Sharon is not passively waiting for final status talks and agreement with a Palestinian leader to determine what will be annexed to Israel: 'Israel is in a building frenzy in the area between the Green Line and the route of the separation fence under cover of America turning a blind eye'.[54] This building frenzy, proceeding even in areas currently undeveloped within the settlement master plans, will ensure the *de facto* annexation of these blocs to Israel regardless of the outcome of negotiations in the future.

Moreover, it is not just major settlement clusters that are included on the Israeli side of the wall but a number of small, sparsely populated settlements. In particular, the route around Zufin and Salit settlements in the Qalqilya district surrounds enormous reserves of land in excess of their master plans, ensuring the future growth of these settlements, while tolling the death knell for the Palestinian villages whose land the wall has isolated (see Chapter 2). It is no coincidence that this area also includes the abundant water reserves of the Western Aquifer, and the acquisition of this land further obliterates the Green Line and widens Israel's narrow 'waist' at one of its most strategic points.

The international community appears to tacitly accept this route, judging by the low-key reaction to the 2005 cabinet decision and the reluctance of states to put pressure on Israel to implement the ICJ advisory opinion. Most presumably do so on the assumption that if the wall defines the new border, at least the Palestinians will end up with the 90 per cent of the West Bank that lies on 'their side'. This figure is not substantially different from what Arafat was offered at Camp David in 2000 (accepting the Israeli/US interpretation of what went on at the summit), which he is widely considered to have been bloody minded, or at least politically unwise, to have rejected. Following Israel's disengagement from the Gaza Strip, the international community will put pressure on Israel for a more comprehensive withdrawal from the West Bank to provide the territorial basis for the Palestinian state the Road Map is intended to achieve.

As the wall assumes the character of a new border, such reasoning goes, the Israeli settlements on the Palestinian side will be prime candidates for removal. It will become obvious to the residents themselves that these settlements have no future, and the estimated 70,000 settlers will have to relocate to the Israeli side of the wall, possibly in exchange for the 49,000 Palestinians presently stranded there. While not denying the injustice to the Palestinians concerned, many of whom would become refugees for a second time – as opposed to the illegal implants, the settlers – this would not constitute a major upheaval compared to, for example, recent population movements in the Balkans, especially if the exchange is underwritten and compensated by the international community.[55] The wall, therefore, this reasoning goes, for all its negative humanitarian consequences in the short-term, will yield political dividends as an instrument for achieving a two-state solution to the conflict by allowing for a Palestinian state to emerge in a truncated West Bank and a 'disengaged' Gaza Strip.[56]

This reasoning is based on the fallacy that if the land currently on the Israeli side of the wall will be formally annexed by Israel in the future, it follows that everything to the east will by default accrue to the Palestinian state. Although the first part of the equation is true, there is no indication that the wall constitutes the final frontier or that Israel's territorial designs are confined to the 10 per cent currently annexed. Sharon himself speaks of continuing Israel's hold on the Jordan Valley and Hebron, areas currently well beyond the current extent of the wall,[57] and other Likud figures to his right are more extreme in their territorial ambitions. While such views may ultimately represent a 'wish list', there is every indication that in return for giving up the Gaza, 'the intention is to fight for every single place' in the West Bank.[58] In this regard, vagueness as to what constitutes the boundaries of a settlement bloc is to Sharon's advantage. As he explained in August 2005, 'The Americans have often asked us to sketch out the boundaries of large settlement blocs in Judea and Samaria [the West Bank], and we have refrained from doing so in the hope that by the time the discussion on the settlement blocs comes, one day, these blocs will contain a very large number of settlements and residents'.[59]

Moreover, today's medium-size settlements or groups of settlements can become tomorrow's blocs due to natural growth and the seeding of 'illegal' outposts. 'Beit El and Ofra are large settlements today with thousands of residents', Sharon declared in an interview in early 2005, referring to settlements strategically located along Route 60 in the central West Bank.[60] In time, in the absence of a peace process and Sharon's genius at creating facts on the ground, these proto-blocs can become the genuine article through the 'natural growth' denied their Palestinian neighbours. Here the 'temporary nature' of the wall becomes a double-edged sword: it can be moved eastwards in future to encompass what has become – because of more facts on the ground in the interim – a new settlement bloc and therefore eligible for future annexation, according to the Bush letter. In this scenario, Shilo-Eli, Beit El–Ofra and their satellites will constitute the new settlement blocs, with future negotiations on the wall (between Israel and the United States, with the Palestinians excluded) focusing not on the Green Line or the existing route but on moving the wall deeper into the West Bank to take into account these 'new realities on the ground'.[61]

NOTES

1. Nahum Barnea and Shimon Shiffer, 'Sharon will show Bush photos: a fence, not a wall', *Yedioth Ahronoth*, 29 July 2003.
2. Nahum Barnea and Shimon Shiffer, 'They bypassed the fence', *Yedioth Ahronoth*, 30 July 2003.
3. Israel Ministry of Defence, *The Seam Zone*, <http://www.seamzone.mod.gov.il/Pages/ENG/default.htm> (accessed on 21 October 2005).
4. Roger Cohen, 'Israel's wall, a victory for the logic of war', *New York Times*, 14 July 2004.
5. Israel Ministry of Foreign Affairs, *The Anti-Terrorist Fence: An Overview*, <http://securityfence.mfa.gov.il/mfm/Data/48152.doc> (accessed on 13 October 2005).
6. Meron Rappaport, 'A wall in the heart', *Yedioth Ahronoth*, 26 May 2003.
7. Doron Almog, *The West Bank Fence: A Vital Component in Israel's Strategy of Defense* (Washington Institute for Near East Policy, April 2004).
8. Amos Harel, 'Security sources: cost of fence could rise to NIS [new Israeli shekels] 15M per km', *Ha'aretz*, 23 February 2004.
9. Amnon Barzilai, 'Changes in separation fence will cost up to NIS 100m', *Ha'aretz*, 7 January 2005. According to Defence Minister Shaul Mofaz, once the barrier is complete, annual maintenance will cost about NIS 170,000 (US$ 40,000) per kilometre, or NIS 85 million (US$ 20 million) in total. Amnon Barzilai, 'Mofaz says fence is good for economy', *Ha'aretz*, 23 June 2004.
10. Yuval Yoaz, 'State to High Court: fence route determined not only by security considerations', *Ha'aretz*, 4 July 2005.
11. *International Court of Justice, Advisory Opinion: Legal Consequences of the Construction of a Wall in the Occupied Palestinian Territory, 9 July 2004*, para. 67. Available online at <http://www.icj-cij.org/icjwww/idocket/imwp/imwpframe.htm> (accessed on 13 October 2005).
12. In anticipation of Israel's evacuation of the Jewish settlements in the Gaza Strip, in June 2005 the Israeli navy began construction of a barrier off the Gaza coastline, consisting primarily of an underwater net, to prevent the infiltration of Palestinians from Gaza into Israel. Arieh O'Sullivan, 'Navy builds terror barrier off Gaza', *Jerusalem Post*, 17 June 2005. The IDF also planned to strengthen the existing barrier around the Strip by building two fences on either side of the existing one, and constructing 'roads for both light vehicles and heavy armored vehicles, as well as sophisticated

monitoring equipment meant to help identify and even fire on approaching threats. Command-and-control centers in the area will supervise and operate the fences and their additional equipment.' Sam Ser, 'IDF building triple fence around Gaza', *Jerusalem Post*, 29 July 2005.

13. Information from B'Tselem, *Behind the Barrier: Human Rights Violations as a Result of Israel's Separation Barrier*, April 2003, pp. 6–7. <http://www.btselem.org/Download/200304_Behind_The_Barrier_Eng.pdf> (accessed on 18 October 2005).

14. 1bid, p. 9.

15. United Nations Office for the Coordination of Humanitarian Affairs (UNOCHA), 'Preliminary analysis of the humanitarian implications of February 2005 barrier projections', February 2005.

16. Nina Gilbert, 'Fence can't be completed until '06', *Jerusalem Post*, 18 February 2005.

17. Amnesty International, *Without Distinction: Attacks on Civilians by Palestinian Armed Groups*, July 2002. Human Rights Watch, *Erased in a Moment: Suicide Bombing Attacks against Israeli Civilians*, October 2002. In November 2004 the UN General Assembly adopted a resolution condemning suicide bombings against Israeli civilians.

18. 'Following the success of the security barrier, we are now witnessing a phenomenon in which terrorists attempt to launch their attacks and infiltrate from areas to the south and to places where the fence has not yet been completed (mainly through Jerusalem and Ramallah).' IDF spokesperson, 7 July 2004. A double suicide attack on buses in Israel's southern city of Beersheba on 31 August 2004 by Hamas militants from Hebron, which resulted in 16 fatalities, was one example of this change in strategy. In all of 2004 there were only two suicide attacks carried out from the northern West Bank as opposed to twelve the previous year, with Israeli fatalities dropping from 74 to 14. Amos Harel, 'Terrorists killed 117 Israelis last year', *Ha'aretz*, 7 January 2005.

19. Yossi Yehoshua and Roni Shaked, 'Drop in terror', *Yedioth Ahronoth*, 23 June 2004.

20. International Court of Justice, *Advisory Opinion*, para. 141.

21. 'A wall as a weapon', *New York Times*, 23 February 2004.

22. Amnon Barzilai, 'Cost of fence could be halved if built along 1967 lines', *Ha'aretz*, 4 February 2004. According to one army source interviewed by the journalist Meron Rappaport, the expense of building the wall deep inside the West Bank to include settlements like Kedumim is such that it 'would be cheaper to give each resident . . . a villa in the

center of Israel than to build this fence'. Rappaport, 'A wall in the heart'.

23. HEPG/LACC, *The Impact of Israel's Separation Barrier on Affected West Bank Communities: A Follow-up Report to Humanitarian and Emergency Policy Group (HEPG) of the Local Aid Coordination Committee (LACC)*, Update Number 3, 31 July 2003, para. 5. The authors caution that '[t]his is not to minimize the economic loss to individual landowners who have seen their lands requisitioned for the barrier's alignment'. For a critique of the concept of building the wall, including what the author terms the 'misguided constructivism' of those who favour a wall along the Green Line, see Andreas Muller, *A Wall on the Green Line*, The Alternative Information Centre, Jerusalem 2004.

24. B'Tselem, *Behind the Barrier*, p. 33.

25. B'Tselem, 'Not all it seems: preventing Palestinian access to their lands west of the separation barrier in the Tulkarm–Qalqilya area', June 2004, p. 6.

26. B'Tselem, *Behind the Barrier*, p. 33.

27. Reserve Brigadier-General Yehuda Golan, quoted in Tovah Lazaroff, 'Generals: fence route is dangerous', *Jerusalem Post*, 30 March 2004.

28. Lily Galili, 'Fence and defense', *Ha'aretz*, 21 March 2004. The military expert quoted is Shaul Givoli, Director-General of the Council for Peace and Security and former Military Governor of Nablus.

29. Ibid. Avraham Bendor-Shalom (former head of Israeli internal intelligence service) concurs: 'So as not to endanger the guards at the passages, thorough – meaning slow – inspections will be necessary. There will be riots and outbursts at every opening every day, and clearly there will be attempts at terrorist attacks, which will kill and maim people. The fence will thus encourage terrorism and attacks.' 'The bad fence', *Ha'aretz*, 28 November 2003.

30. Galili, 'Fence and defense'.

31. B'Tselem, *Under the Guise of Security: Case Study: The Zufin Settlement*, <http://www.btselem.org/Download/200509_Guise_of_Security_Case_Study_Zufin_Eng.doc> (accessed on 21 October 2005).

32. B'Tselem, *Behind the Barrier*, p. 33.

33. Henry Siegman, 'Israel: the threat from within', *New York Review of Books*, 6 February 2004.

34. B'Tselem, *Behind the Barrier*, p. 34.

35. Rappaport, 'A wall in the heart'. 'Security sources involved in the fence's construction confirm that this was the order, and that the first maps were drawn accordingly.'

36. B'Tselem, *The Separation Barrier*, p. 33.

37. Mazal Mualem, 'Fence-sitting', *Ha'aretz*, 31 May 2003.

38. Shlomo Brom, 'The security fence: solution or stumbling block?" Strategic Assessment, the Jaffee Center for Strategic Studies, February 2004, p. 9. Regarding support for the wall, a survey in March 2004 revealed that 'Despite the domestic and foreign criticism of the separation fence, the Israeli-Jewish public almost unanimously (84 per cent) supports it (13 per cent oppose it and 3 per cent do not know). The wide public support for the fence crosses the political parties.' Ephraim Yaar and Tamar Hermann, 'Peace index: most Israelis support the fence, despite Palestinian suffering', *Ha'aretz*, 10 March 2004.

39. 'Military sources . . . said recently that every question that comes up goes to the Prime Minister's Office, to Sharon's adviser on settler affairs, Uzi Keren, and to Sharon himself.' Rappaport, 'A wall in the heart'.

40. In practice, this has resulted in the wall being built without the customary feasibility or impact studies one would expect for such an important project. 'There is a noticeable absence of comprehensive and ongoing control and oversight by the civilian establishment, whose task it is to examine the far-reaching implications of Israel's largest infrastructure project for national security and the state's interests.' Kobi Michael and Amnon Ramon, *A Fence Around Jerusalem* (Jerusalem, The Jerusalem Institute for Israel Studies, 2004), p. 16

41. Quoted in Rappaport, 'A wall in the heart'.

42. Ibid.

43. Nadav Shragai, 'Fence proposal fires controversy among settler leaders', *Ha'aretz*, 4 February 2003.

44. Rappaport, 'A Wall in the heart'.

45. Shaul Yaholom of the settler-dominated National Religious Party, acting chairman of the Knesset committee overseeing the defence budget, explained his refusal to approve funding for a route that didn't encompass settlements: 'Anyone who expects me to abandon tens of thousands of residents of Ariel and Maale Adumim will be disappointed.' Bradley Burston, 'Fence divides Israel and US, Israeli and Israeli', *Ha'aretz*, 17 September 2003.

46. The journalist Akiva Eldar describes attending a lecture delivered by Sharon in 2001: 'He removed a large map of the land of Israel . . . and pointed to the areas he proposed annexing to Israel. The pointer in his hand went from the Ariel bloc deep in Samaria to greater Jerusalem, and from there to the Etzion bloc and Hebron. Then the pointer hovered over

the Jordan Valley, from Bet Shean to the Dead Sea. These regions, Sharon explained, are vital for Israel's security. They must not be conceded even in return for the best of peace arrangements.' Akiva Eldar, 'In the eye of the beholder', *Bitterlemons*, 14 June 2004. <http://www.bitterlemons.org/previous/bl140604ed21.html#is2> (accessed on 21 October 2005).

47. Rappaport, 'A wall in the heart'.

48. Amnon Barzilai, 'PM adviser: no plans for "eastern fence" in West Bank', *Ha'aretz*, 10 March 2004. '"The State of Israel will not build a separation fence in the eastern part of the West Bank because of the diplomatic damage it is likely to endure as a result," said Colonel (res.) Dan Tirza, who is considered the most senior professional adviser to Prime Minister Ariel Sharon on the issue of the fence. "Legally and publicly, the building of the separation fence in the eastern sector is likely to cause serious damage to the state," he said. "So we shouldn't invest money in it."'

49. 'Back to the fence', *Ha'aretz*, 8 September 2004.

50. Itamar Eichner, 'Fence approved', *Yedioth Ahronoth*, 2 October 2003. Yossi Sarid, who had originally supported the idea of a wall, came to regret his decision. 'If Sharon is able to take something straight and twist it out of shape, he will unquestionably do so. At the time I even warned Haim Ramon [of the Labour Party] and the other fence advocates that, when it was built, they would have a hard time recognizing their original intent, and that we would come to regret our support for it, just as many people have come to regret their support for various Sharon initiatives over the years, having always come out on the short end of the stick.' Yossi Sarid, 'My affidavit to The Hague', *Ha'aretz*, 21 January 2004.

51. International Court of Justice, *Advisory Opinion*, paras. 119, 137.

52. Text of letter from President Bush to Prime Minister Sharon, 15 April 2004.

53. 'His aides say that he did so with much pain. That it was hard for him to give up the expansive, gorgeous region, where only a thousand or so Bedouin live with their herds, and leave it outside the fence. But the land is being worked, mainly as pasture, and after the High Court decision, the legal advisers are opposed to leaving landholdings of Palestinians on the Israeli side.' Aluf Benn, 'Israel's new frontier', *Ha'aretz*, 25 February 2005.

54. Aluf Benn, 'Drawing the line', *Ha'aretz*, 25 March 2005.

55. 'In order to make the withdrawal from additional settlements on the other side of the barrier more politically palatable, Sharon must begin driving home the message that such a partial withdrawal can be carried out only in the quid pro quo context of a population exchange in which Palestinian villages will be removed from the western side of the barrier. Pushing such a policy is daunting but not impossible, and must be aimed primarily at American policy makers and public opinion.' Yosef Goell, 'The missing link', *Jerusalem Post*, 21 February 2005.

56. This is the argument of the US academic George Gavrilis, who maintains that '[a]lthough the prevailing view of the fence is that it is a tool of Israeli territorial expansion, the barrier alternatively can be seen as a tool of exclusion that leaves out many of Israel's most radical and isolated settlements and by definition pushes them outside the boundaries of a future Israeli state'. 'Sharon's endgame for the West Bank barrier', *The Washington Quarterly*, Autumn 2004, pp. 9–10.

57. See the Sharon interviews, David Horovitz and Herb Keinon, 'Sharon speaks to the "*Post*"', *Jerusalem Post*, 22 April 2005; Aluf Benn and Yossi Verter, 'Even King Solomon ceded territories', *Ha'aretz*, 22 April 2004.

58. Ari Shavit, 'The big freeze', *Ha'aretz*, 8 October 2004.

59. Shahar Illan, 'Sharon against the haters from Tel Aviv', *Ha'aretz*, 25 August 2005.

60. Horovitz and Keinon, 'Sharon speaks to the "*Post*"'.

61. 'The Shilo–Eli "bloc" today numbers 15 unauthorized outposts, all of them located on hills east and west of the settlements of Shilo and Eli. The objective: a linking up of Shilo and Eli westward to Ariel and eastward to the Allon road in the Jordan Valley. The Itamar–Yitzhar "bloc" numbers 16 unauthorized outposts whose purpose is to link up the bloc to the Jordan Valley. The same story in the Beit El–Ofra "bloc", which today numbers ten unauthorized outposts whose purpose is to link up the two established settlements to the Jordan Valley.' Oded Shalom, 'The day after the pullout', *Yedioth Ahronoth*, 23 April 2004.

Hydrologist Abdul-Latif Khaled holds up the permits and ID cards he needs to pass through various wall gates daily for his work, Jayous, West Bank

2 'The Land Without the People'

The Impact of the Wall

'A DRAMATIC INCREASE IN THE QUALITY OF LIFE'

At the United Nations headquarters in New York on 9 July 2004, Israel's Permanent Representative, Dan Gillerman, was holding a press conference. The International Court of Justice had just delivered its advisory opinion, 'a dark day for the International Court of Justice and the international legal system', Ambassador Gillerman declared. The ICJ ruled that the wall – where it deviated into the West Bank and East Jerusalem, which was for the majority of its route – was contrary to international law. Israel must cease construction, dismantle the sections already built, compensate those affected and 'repeal or render ineffective' the gate and permit system.

Apart from legal arguments, the judges had heard testimony about the devastating impact that the completed sections of the wall were having on Palestinian communities in the northern West Bank. Qalqilya City was cut off from its hinterland and facing social and economic stagnation. Rural communities were separated from the land and water resources on which they depended for their livelihood. The situation was especially acute for Palestinians isolated in closed areas between the wall and the Green Line who required special permits to reside in their homes and to access educational and health services on the Palestinian side of the wall. As a result of all these restrictions Palestinians were beginning to leave these wall-affected areas, 'a process that will continue', the ICJ warned, 'as more of the wall is built'.[1] Yet, for all this evidence to the contrary, Gillerman claimed that an important consequence of the wall was 'a dramatic increase in the quality of life and humanitarian situation of Palestinians in the areas through which it ran'.[2]

It was true that there had been an improvement in the Palestinian economy compared to the early years of the second *intifada*, when military incursions and stringent restrictions on the movement of people and goods had devastated social and economic life. The World Bank reported a 'marginal improvement in per capita incomes' in 2003, but they were still 36 per cent lower than their pre-*intifada* levels, and indicators for the first part of 2004 revealed the economy stagnant again. Almost half of the Palestinian population was living below the official poverty line of just over $US2 a day, and 16 per cent of Palestinians were living in absolute poverty, barely surviving despite significant provisions of humanitarian assistance.[3] An assessment by the UN Food and Agriculture Organization found that approximately 40 per cent of the population was 'food insecure' and that this insecurity was high in regions previously known for their agricultural abundance: the Jenin, Tulkarm and Qalqilya districts where the wall was already constructed.[4] The two biggest food providers in the region, the UN Relief and Works Agency for Palestine Refugees (UNRWA) and the UN World Food Programme – who between them were providing food aid to almost 1.5 million Palestinians in 2004 – had conducted surveys that corroborated these findings.[5] UNICEF, the UN Children's Fund, also reported 'an increase in chronic malnutrition and a degradation of the nutritional status of small children' and warned that 'one in ten children under five is now suffering from stunting'.[6] Indeed, such was the 'humanitarian food crisis' that the UN Special Rapporteur on the Right to Food, Jean Ziegler, advocated that the European Union suspend its Association Agreement with Israel, because of Israel's failure to respect the Agreement's humans rights clauses.[7]

The negative impact of the wall was well known to Marouf Zahran, the mayor of Qalqilya in the Northern West Bank. Situated on rich land and water reserves, the city had been a major agricultural producer as well as a commercial and service centre for the 32 villages in the Qalqilya district, until its encirclement by the wall in late 2003. Unemployment had risen to 75 per cent and over 600 out of 1,800 commercial establishments had closed down. More than 4,000 of Qalqilya's 43,000 citizens had migrated to other West Bank towns: a drive through the once vibrant commercial area of the city revealed workshops and stores shuttered up. Residents were unable to pay their municipal taxes and the Israeli Electric Company was threatening to cut off the city's supply. Thousands of families were surviving on social assistance, and the pressure was taking its toll on civil life with families split, divorces and criminality rising, and children showing symptoms of psychological trauma. Worst for Zahran, a political moderate known for his support for peace initiatives and contacts with Israelis, the frustration has led to a rise in support for militant groups such as Hamas and Islamic Jihad.

The city's travails date back well before the construction of the wall, to the creation of the State of Israel in 1948. Its location less than 20 kilometres from the Mediterranean would have been an advantage in a less conflict-prone region but proved a liability due to its proximity to Israel's narrow 'waist'. Qalqilya repulsed the advances of the Alexandroni Brigade in the 1948 Arab-Israeli war, but border adjustments following the end of hostilities resulted in the loss of 80 per cent of its farmland. Thousands of refugees from what would become the state of Israel fled to Qalqilya and their descendants make up 70 per cent of the population today. Qalqilya became a border town, close to the burgeoning Tel Aviv metropolitan area and perceived by Israel as a threatening salient jutting into the Jewish state. Nevertheless, the city recovered and thrived in the following decades, becoming a major agricultural producer on land cleared for cultivation to replace the territory lost to Israel. Its recovery was helped by its location on the Western Aquifer, the largest water source in the region, which allowed for the drilling of new artesian wells and the practice of intensive agriculture.

In the 1967 Arab-Israeli war, Qalqilya suffered heavy aerial and tank bombardment and 70 per cent of the city was destroyed. Those who had not fled the hostilities were rounded up by the IDF and bussed to the Jordan border. Residents feared that they would suffer the same fate as the Latrun salient to the south, where three villages were levelled and their inhabitants permanently expelled. Fortunately, after several weeks most were allowed to return to Qalqilya due to the intervention of the UN Security Council, although many who were expelled to Jordan remain in exile to this day.

Immediately after the occupation, the Israeli authorities imposed quotas on existing wells and restricted drilling for agricultural use: only 23 permits for new wells were granted between 1967 and 1990 for the whole West Bank, 20 of which were for domestic use.[8] By contrast, the drilling of groundwater wells increased along the part of the Western Aquifer located in Israel: seven deep wells were drilled on the Israeli side of Qalqilya alone. The Jewish settlements mushrooming through-

[74]

out the West Bank were integrated into the Israeli water carrier system, Mekorot, through pipes and pumping stations.[9] Qalqilya's rich land and water resources and its proximity to the Tel Aviv metropolitan area made the district an obvious target for Israeli settlement. By 2000, 19 settlements with an estimated population of 50,000 had been established throughout the Qalqilya district, accounting for 25 per cent of all settlers in the West Bank.

The occupation had the result of integrating the Israeli and Palestinian economies, albeit to the advantage of the more developed occupying power. Large numbers of Palestinians from the Qalqilya district flocked to the Israeli labour market while Israelis benefited from access to the cheaper goods and services across the defunct Green Line. Although the number of Palestinian day labourers declined sharply after the first *intifada* in the late 1980s, 6,000 workers from Qalqilya City continued to commute to Israel. Israeli Arabs cultivated business and trade links with their West Bank counterparts, and in the 'Oslo years' 42 joint business ventures were set up between Qalqilya and Israeli partners.

The outbreak of the second *intifada* in late 2000 marked the end of this relative prosperity. Access to jobs in Israel ceased and income from commerce and manufacturing plummeted. A policy of strict internal closure fragmented the West Bank, restricting the access of residents of the hinterland villages to Qalqilya and the ability of the city's traders to transport goods to markets elsewhere in the West Bank.[10] Although the role of agriculture as an earner for the city diminished, its importance as a 'shock absorber' for the newly unemployed increased, with 2,000 agricultural workers supporting 15,000 residents by 2003. Deprived of its role as a regional commercial centre, Qalqilya could still have survived on its own agricultural resources but the wall put paid to that.

Of the city's remaining 6,000 dunams of agricultural land, almost 5,000 are occupied by the wall and its flanking obstacles, or isolated in closed areas, as are agricultural wells supplying a third of the city's water. Since October 2003, access to these land and water resources has been dependent on the gate and permit regime. Only 400 such permits were initially delivered to the Qalqilya municipality, with hundreds of landowners denied them. Once the initial permits expired, landowners were obliged to apply to the Civil Administration – the civilian face of the military occupation in the West Bank – for renewal. To qualify, applicants had to furnish updated land ownership documents, official certification that these documents were valid, and a 'magnetic card' to testify that the holder did not pose a security risk. Certifying ownership of land proved particularly difficult given the confused land ownership system in the West Bank and the custom of landowners bequeathing land to several sons without formally registering the change of ownership.[11] Landless labourers who were initially issued permits were now rejected, inflicting a serious loss of income on the poorest strata of rural society. The allocation of permits in Qalqilya still stood at approximately 30 per cent of applicants by early 2005, leading to a decline in agricultural productivity and food production as land, crops and orchards in the closed areas went neglected and untended.

Like many Palestinians in communities affected by the wall, Mayor Zahran would reluctantly have accepted a barrier along the Green Line to seal off Qalqilya City from Israel. He accepts that Palestinians bear their share of responsibility for the bloodletting of the second *intifada* and that a number of suicide bombers have originated from his city. However, neither he nor his co-residents understand the security logic of a wall that 'tightens a noose' around Qalqilya, cutting the city off not just from Israel but from neighbouring Palestinian villages and isolating the land and water resources on which its livelihood depends. As mayor, he understands better than most that such a wall will not bring security, instead engendering frustration, hopelessness and a rise in support for extremism and militancy.[12] However, as described in the previous chapter, it was not Mayor Zahran but his neighbour to the south, the head of the Alfei Menashe settlement, who determined the route of the wall in the Qalqilya area with such disastrous consequences for Qalqilya City and the surrounding villages.

International criticism of the impact of the wall on Palestinians has belatedly compelled Israel to introduce measures to ease restrictions. A system of tunnels and underpasses is planned throughout the West Bank to restore transport links and services to beleaguered communities. The first was completed in 2004, restoring direct passage between Qalqilya and the villages to its south which had been severed by the wall. Mayor Zahran concedes that the Qalqilya tunnel has allowed his citizens 'to breathe' and has led to some revival in the city's fortunes: by early 2005, unemployment was down to 64 per cent and the exodus from the city has slowed down. However, the tunnel is only tolerated as a short-term and local measure, pending the dismantling of the wall as demanded by the ICJ. It is not acceptable as a link in a new discriminatory transport system that will enable settlers to travel without restriction on new, state-of-the art roads while Palestinians are confined to underpasses and secondary networks. In any case, the 'transportation contiguity' these tunnels provide, though improving social and economic conditions in the short term, will not reconnect communities such as Qalqilya to the land and water resources on which their long-term survival depends.

Nor does the current wall mark the end of the city's misfortune, for the long, invasive section to be built around the 'Ariel Finger' will eviscerate what is left of the Qalqilya district to the east. All the settlements, of which the district has a disproportionate share, will be enclosed by the wall, leaving the Palestinian communities with few land and water resources. Surveying a map of the Qalqilya district criss-crossed by a serpentine wall, Mayor Zahran is adamant that no Palestinian leader can accept such a 'bantustan', a statelet without land or water reserves, or real sovereignty. He fears that Qalqilya may be the prototype for a future Palestine of decaying towns caged in by concrete slabs and electronic fences, linked by tunnels or underpasses to depleted hinterlands.

As evidence of Sharon's real intentions for his city, Zahran cites the fact that plans to create an industrial zone have been rejected by the Israeli authorities although donor funding is available. The city's proximity to the Mediterranean ports make it an obvious location for a project that could provide work for the thousands cut off by the wall from the Israeli labour market and from their agricultural land. For lack of such enterprises, Qalqilya's young people are drifting away to other West Bank cities, or like the Mayor's own son, are emigrating. By inducing a 'voluntary transfer' of the young and the educated, Marouf Zahran fears that the wall may yet accomplish in Qalqilya what the Israeli army failed to do in 1948 and in 1967.

'THEY STOLE THE SMILE FROM OUR FACES'

While Qalqilya City was in social and economic decline as a result of the 'hijacking' of the route for the benefit of the settlers, its neighbouring villages were facing similar problems. To the south, five Palestinian villages were cut off in a closed area, victims of the success of the Mayor of Alfei Menashe in having his settlement located on the 'Israeli side' of the wall. Since October 2003, the 1,200 Palestinian inhabitants of these villages have become 'long-term' or 'permanent residents', requiring permits to reside in their own homes, in breach of an assurance which Ambassador Gillerman had given to the UN Security Council that their legal status would remain unchanged.[13] Access to health and educational facilities is severely disrupted, as these services are located on the 'Palestinian side' of the wall. The new regime has also severely disrupted extended family and social networks, with relatives and friends requiring special permits to visit the closed areas. In addition, the wall has reconfigured local geography so that another three neighbouring villages are semi-isolated, their 7,500 inhabitants cut off both from nearby Qalqilya City and the five closed-area villages.[14]

Located on the cusp of the two enclaves is the co-educational school in Ras Atiya built with World Bank and Swiss funding. The headmaster, Mohammed Shaheen, was used to coping with movement restrictions even before the arrival of the wall. Twenty of his 25 teachers lived outside the village, and the checkpoints, earth mounds and other obstacles often resulted in their arriving late or not at all. Loss of teaching time resulted in a decline in educational standards and the reassigning of several teachers to schools closer to their homes; all told, the Palestinian Ministry of Education had to relocate some 15,000 out of its 27,000 teacher workforce during the course of the second *intifada*.[15] In September 2002, to ensure that the textbooks arrived in time for the school year, Shaheen transported the books by horse and cart from Qalqilya, finishing the journey by donkey when the horse balked at passing through a drainage tunnel.

Such obstacles paled before the problems the wall posed. Shortly after that school year started, Shaheen learnt that the route would pass within ten metres of his school. His requests to the Civil Administration that the wall be moved a 100 metres away were refused on security grounds. Teaching was disrupted by the noise of explosives used to clear the ground, and cracks appeared in the school walls. Schoolboys threw stones at the security guards and the IDF threatened to demolish the school if the disruption continued. A peaceful protest by locals and international activists was broken up by teargas and residents were warned that the village would be placed under indefinite curfew if demonstrations continued.[16] Fading slogans in English on the perimeter walls bear testimony to these solidarity protests: 'Let me learn peacefully'; 'UNESCO, where are you?' In the end the route went ahead as planned and another quiet rural village found itself threatened by the new frontier.

With the completion of the wall the five small communities to the east of Ras Atiya were isolated in a closed area, cut off from Qalqilya city, the regional hub, and from villages such as Ras Atiya on which they depend for education and health services. The one elementary school in the enclave, in Daba'a, catered only to grade seven: some 260 pupils had to travel out of the enclave each day, including 40 to the Ras Atiya school. Conversely, eight teachers from outside the enclave required permits to reach their school in Dab'a; as a concession their names were placed on a list to be checked daily by the soldiers at the gate. This movement was initially negotiated through two gates, which often remained closed on Saturdays and on Jewish holidays. On most days, long delays were common as pupils waited for the soldiers bearing the key to arrive, and were then subject to humiliating searches.[17] With funding from Canada, the Palestinian Authority Ministry of Education constructed additional classrooms in the Dab'a school. In light of the negative publicity generated by children queuing, the Israeli authorities provided a bus to transport the pupils into and out of the enclave.

The Palestinian villages trapped within the Alfei Menashe enclave are not connected to electricity or water networks, and so are dependent on generators and on cisterns and water tankers. There are no medical services, and residents depend on the vagaries of the gate opening times to reach medical facilities located outside the enclave. They also rely on the weekly visits of mobile health clinics, whose personnel themselves require permits to enter the closed area. Since the gates are not manned around the clock, these restrictions pose a particular problem for expectant mothers and for emergency and chronic cases.[18] The first fatality directly attributable to the wall was a two-year-old child from Ras Atiya, who was suddenly taken ill with fever. A local doctor referred him to a hospital in Qalqilya, but as no soldiers were present to open the Hable gate, the parents were forced on a long detour to rendezvous with a waiting ambulance, and the child died before reaching hospital.[19]

During the second *intifada*, the Palestinian Authority Ministry of Health responded to similar movement restrictions by increasing the number of primary health care facilities and mobile clinics, and by reallocating services such as dialysis machines to more remote areas. However, such decentralisation brings with it a decline in the quality of care and is not economically sustainable in the long term. That the wall will result in a further decline in the quality of service appears inevitable: a study of wall-affected areas found that only 48 per cent of doctors live in the same or neighbouring village as their heath centre, increasing 'local reliance on nurses and health workers relative to trained physicians'.[20]

Despite the problems the wall poses for health and education services Palestinians cite 'separation from relatives' as their main complaint, 'well ahead of the increased price of goods, agricultural problems and forced displacement'.[21] Again it is the gate and permit regime that is responsible: all Palestinians above the age of twelve who want to visit family members or friends in the closed areas require permits, with special permission needed to stay overnight.[22] Residents of the closed areas now habitually celebrate religious festivals, as well as weddings, funerals, birthdays and similar occasions, without the presence of their extended families. Lacking a permit, Mohammed Shaheen has not been to the villages in the Alfei Menashe enclave since completion of the wall, not even to visit the mourning houses of the deceased relatives of his pupils which, under normal circumstances, would be considered unpardonable for one of his respected social standing. In the 'Barta'a enclave' in Jenin, the largest Palestinian community cut off within a closed area, parents worry whether their sons will be able to marry; it is the custom for a new wife to move to her husband's locality and, as the mayor explained 'nobody wants to send their daughter to a prison'.[23]

Women, who during the second *intifada* have faced 'increased demands as care-givers and providers while at the same time their freedom of movement and action has been curtailed', bear the brunt of these new movement restrictions.[24] Families are increasingly reluctant to allow female members, including girl pupils, to endure the humiliating delays and searches at the gates, further diminishing women's mobility, social participation and educational opportunities. Children's social and recreational activities are also affected by the wall. Palestinian pupils from the five villages within the Alfei Menashe enclave cannot participate in extra-curricular activities in the Ras Atiya school for fear of missing the final gate opening time. As Mohammed Shaheen explains, the school declined an invitation to participate in a middle-distance running competition in nearby Tulkarm: parents were reluctant to send their children, and in any case, where would the pupils find the space to train in the confined space of the semi-enclave?

More difficult to assess is the psychological impact of the wall, on children especially, particularly against the background of pervasive violence which has characterised the second *intifada*.[25] A survey found that almost half of children had personally experienced conflict-related violence or witnessed violence affecting a member of their immediate family. In the same survey, 90 per cent of parents reported symptomatic traumatic behaviour in their children, ranging from nightmares and bedwetting, to increased aggressiveness and hyperactivity, and a decrease in attention span and concentration.[26] A preliminary study of wall-related symptoms in the Qalqilya area found 'a high prevalence of depressive factors apparent in sleeping and eating disorders as well as psycho-somatic symptoms among adults and children'.[27] Morale among all ages is further undermined by the failure of non-violent protests to stop the wall or to lessen the impact of the route, and uncertainty about what declining economic conditions mean for the future of affected communities.

The threat to livelihoods results from the wall's impact on agricultural practice. The Civil Administration's failure to provide conveniently located agricultural gates means that farmers from Dab'a have to travel more than ten kilometres to reach their lands outside the enclave, with a consequent decline in cultivation and productivity. Shepherds in the three Bedouin communities within the enclave have been forced to sell their sheep due to lack of land for grazing and money for fodder. Losing their source of livelihood, their alternatives are either 'illegal entry into Israel' or 'temporary work for starvation wages in the settlement of Alfei Menashe as menial laborers of the Jewish settlers', in the words of a petition filed on behalf of the communities by the Association for Civil Rights in Israel (ACRI).[28]

Insecurity of residency and the knowledge that Alfei Menashe settlement will expand and take over what little village land remains add to the uncertainty regarding their future. For three of the communities, their Israeli-issued ID

'They stole the smile from our faces': children's views of the wall. [29]

In November 2003, Save the Children UK carried out research with children in three schools in communities where the wall is already in operation: Azun Atmeh, Ras Atiya and A-Ras in Qalqilya district. A total of 192 ten to twelve-year-olds participated in drama workshops, performing a play, and in class discussions about what is good and bad about the wall, whether they feel more or less secure and what messages they want to pass on. The results showed that children have a well-developed understanding of their rights, and see the wall as denying them those rights. As one child put it, 'it prevents us from the most beautiful thing we own which is our childhood'. There was an alarming rise in children's sense of insecurity and risk from violence, and a growing feeling of injustice to which they have increasingly violent responses. In the words of one child, 'they stole the smile from our faces'.

Children were asked to write down words that describe the wall. The most common word they used to describe the wall was 'a prison'. One child described it as 'a snake that spreads its poison', reflecting the way the wall twists through farmland to encircle the village. Other common terms included images of fear, death and sadness, for example: 'It destroyed our lives', it is 'a deadly barrier' and 'it breaks my heart'.

Children were asked to say what was good about the wall. Few were able to express positive ideas. Of the 132 children participating, only two mentioned that it protects people from suicide attacks, while others ridiculed the concept of the wall being good, with sardonic comments such as 'It prevents our donkey from running far', and 'It prevents invaders from invading my village'.

cards designate locations outside the enclave as their place of origin. The fear is that at some point the Civil Administration will refuse to renew their permanent-resident permits on the grounds that their true place of residence lies elsewhere: according to residents of one of the Bedouin communities, the Civil Administration is already trying to persuade them to move.[30] Discriminatory regulations also prevent their constructing new houses or adding extensions to existing structures: four of the five communities lie within the Oslo-era designation 'Area C', meaning that Israeli approval is needed for all construction. As these permits are rarely granted, most of the buildings in Dab'a and the three Bedouin communities, including sheep pens and water tanks, have been constructed 'illegally' and are under threat of demolition.

Meanwhile, as these communities atrophy, plans for the expansion of Alfei Menashe – the real illegal presence under international law – are well advanced. The master plan envisages the settlement doubling in size – from 2,000 to 4,700 dunams – and the creation of two satellite extensions, Ilanit and Nof Hasharon, to expand the bloc all the way westwards to the Green Line. The circuitous route around the Ras Atiya enclave is designed to ensure that the two new settler satellites will fall on the Israeli side of the wall: according to B'Tselem 'major parts of the route were set with the expansion plans . . . in mind'.[31] In addition, plans for a new twelve-kilometre-long settler bypass road – which will involve the expropriation of thousands more dunams of land from Ras Atiya, Dab'a and other Palestinian villages – will link Alfei Menashe and its satellites, together with the settlements of Karnei Shomron, Kedumim and Imanuel, to the Green Line and to Israel proper.

In its petition to the High Court, ACRI argued that it was because of this desire to keep 'the Jewish settlement of Alfei

Menashe and its undeveloped municipal land to the west of the barrier' that the five Palestinian communities within the enclave were condemned to 'a miserable existence of economic, social, and cultural atrophy'. Arguing, that the route 'was a result of political pressure and has nothing whatsoever to do with security considerations', ACRI demanded that the wall be dismantled and moved to the Green Line, maintaining that 'the barrier, in its present route generates a process of "voluntary" population transfer'.[32]

In its response to the petition, the State Prosecutor denied that the Palestinian residents of the enclave are harmed by the wall. On the contrary 'they benefit from it', in finding it easier to obtain work in the Alfei Menashe settlement, an important advantage in view of 'the widespread unemployment' in the area. As evidence for his claim, the State Prosecutor cited the fact that three of the five communities did not join the petition, demonstrating their satisfaction with the wall.

The ACRI attorney, Michael Sefarad was not alone in finding the state's arguments – with its overtones of Ambassador Gillerman's claims at the United Nations – 'outrageous'. 'Anyone familiar with the appalling conditions in the enclave closed in by the separation walls knows that the residents' lives are very difficult,' Sefarad pointed out. It was not satisfaction that prevented them from joining the petition, but 'their fear of the authorities [which] often deters them from fighting for their rights'.[33]

Despite the State Prosecutor's claims, the High Court agreed to hear the case. For the hearing, ACRI prepared a study in coordination with the Israeli planning rights group, Bimkom, whose experts, including world-renowned architect Moshe Safdie, argued that the route around the enclave was constructed 'without any planning-spatial logic whatsoever to justify its construction'.[34] Equally important, the High Court justices agreed to consider the petition in the context of the International Court of Justice's advisory opinion, as that section of the wall had already been completed when the ICJ deliberated the case. The fate of the five villages therefore depended on the Israeli High Court, with the ruling either leading to a realignment of the wall or a legitimisation of the already constructed route, a route, Bimkom argued, '[that] could lead to the abandonment of the villages and the end of the existence of these communities'.[35]

In a judgement delivered in September 2005, the High Court justices agreed with the petitioners that the route around the Alfei Menashe settlement 'creates a chokehold around the villages [and] severely injures the entire fabric of life'.[36] The justices found the current route 'strange' and were 'not convinced that there is a security-military reason to include in the enclave the three villages in its southwest part, instead of keeping them beyond the fence'.[37] The court therefore ruled that the state, within a reasonable timeframe, must consider an alternative, shorter, route that would remove the Palestinian villagers from the Israeli side of the wall.

Attorney Sefarad welcomed the ruling as 'very brave', in that it had 'saved five Palestinian villages from utter annihilation'.[38] He also believed that the decision would limit the expanse of the route in other areas, including in the Ariel Finger: ironically, in the aftermath of the ruling, the head of one of the Ariel Finger settlements of Karnei Shomron complained that his settlement might 'wither away' if it did not include enough additional land for 'natural growth'.[39] However, in contravention of the ICJ opinion, the High Court ruled, as it had in its earlier Beit Sourik decision, that Israel had the authority to build the wall beyond the Green Line inside the West Bank. It also rejected the petitioners' claim that the wall was built for political rather than security reasons, despite accepting that the route had in part been planned for future expansion rather than the present security of Alfei Menashe settlement. It was not surprising therefore that, despite the loss of some land for future settlement expansion, the head of the Alfei Menashe local council Eliezer Hasdai welcomed the decision as 'a dream', for Alfei Menashe would remain on the Israeli side of the wall, now 'officially part of the State of Israel'.[40]

'A NICE PALESTINIAN VILLAGE'

The fence snakes through in a very interesting way, and crosses through very interesting areas: Here there is a nice Palestinian village, with agricultural lands and access to them, and suddenly they have nothing.

(Colin Powell)[41]

It is not only communities cut off entirely or in part that are in danger of withering away because the wall restricts their access to resources and services and causes a draining away of their population. Also at risk are the far greater number of villages located on the Palestinian side of the wall whose agricultural land is cut off in closed areas on the Israeli side. Although their access to health and education services is largely unaffected, their livelihood is threatened due to farmers' lack of access to their land and water resources as a result of the new gate and permit regime. One of the villages so affected is Jayous in the Qalqilya district, a village of 3,200 inhabitants. Here, the wall intrudes six kilometres in from the Green Line, to within 30 metres of the village houses. As was the case with the Alfei Menashe enclave, the route was determined with future expansion of a settlement in mind, including the creation of an industrial zone.[42] As a result, almost all of the village's cultivated land – including thousands of olive and fruit trees and scores of greenhouses – lies in a closed area on the Israeli side of the wall.

Like most Green Line communities Jayous lost much of its ancestral land in the Arab-Israeli war of 1948, and since 1967 has been waging a constant battle against Israel's attempts to divest it of what remains. Zufin settlement was created in the late 1980s on village land, and a privately owned Israeli quarry shaved off another 400 dunams in 1990. What appears to be a small hill near the southern entrance of the village is where municipal garbage from local Jewish settlements was dumped throughout the 1990s. Smouldering rubbish from this unregulated landfill blanketed Jayous for years, until the settlers in Zufin complained that it was spoiling their environment.

It was not just the land that was under threat of confiscation but the village's water resources. The reason for the fertility of Jayous – and of the north western Green Line communities in general – is its location above the Western Aquifer: 142 wells in the Tulkarm and Qalqilya districts account for total Palestinian extraction of the aquifer for agriculture and drinking needs.[43] All of Jayous's six agricultural wells now lie on the Israeli side of the wall, with access restricted to a single gate. Water for domestic consumption, pumped from a well shared with a neighbouring village, is also affected by Israeli restrictions. At just 23 litres per capita per day, domestic consumption in Jayous is far below the World Health Organization's recommended 100 litres, let alone the 350 litres per capita consumption in Israel and in the settlements.[44] As a result, Jayous suffers critical water shortages in the long summer months, necessitating the purchase of expensive tankered water on the part of householders.

The farmers have withstood this onslaught as best they could. In 1988, when 1,350 dunams of land were confiscated for the creation of Zufin settlement, 80 farmers appealed to the Israeli High Court. Over time, because of the torturous and costly legal process, many dropped out. One who persisted was Shareef Omar, or 'Abu Azzam', the largest landowner in Jayous. Land that lies uncultivated has often been declared 'state property' by the Israeli authorities, utilising an old Ottoman law, and used to build Jewish settlements. Abu Azzam poured money and resources into his threatened 60 dunams, planting olive trees and assiduously tending the land. Hundreds of his olive trees were burnt down, allegedly by collaborators, and he had many confrontations with the soldiers. But in the end, his persistence paid off. In 1996 the High Court ruled that Abu Azzam and the 60 others who had stayed the course could keep their land.

During these, the 'Oslo years', Jayous prospered. Although water for domestic use was limited, the agricultural wells allowed for intensive cultivation. Tomato and cucumber, avocado and mango, almond and fig, guava and peach were cultivated on the fertile soil. The 120 greenhouses that Jayous shares with the neighbouring village of Falamya produced 7 million kilograms of vegetables and fruit annually and each greenhouse could support an entire family. Wholesale merchants would come from Qalqilya and Nablus and from inside Israel to buy the produce directly from the farmers. However, the imposition of a policy of complete closure from the beginning of the second *intifada* cut off much of the domestic Palestinian and all of the Israeli market. Access to the labour market in Israel was also restricted, with the result that most families became totally dependant on agriculture and many of those still employed relied on family land to supplement their income.

And then came the wall. In September 2002, a shepherd found a military summons attached to an olive tree, instructing farmers to assemble for a tour of the projected route. Most villagers had no real notion of what the wall signified and were expecting it to run along the Green Line, as no suicide bombers had originated from Jayous or from neighbouring villages. To their horror, the IDF revealed that the wall would intrude six kilometres from the Green Line right up to the village houses. Shortly after, farmers found more notices pinned to trees, the official requisition orders identifying the plots of land to be seized. Landowners were given one week to appeal to the Military Commander, a deadline that most found impossible to meet given the expense involved in hiring a lawyer and the difficulty in providing the required documents. In any case, a reversal of the original decision was unlikely as the Appeals Committee is part of the same body, the IDF, which had issued the requisition notice in the first place.[45] Some villagers did employ a lawyer, but their appeal was rejected on the grounds of military necessity. By the end of November 2002 land levelling had begun and 4,000 trees were uprooted. For want of space, farmers replanted olive trees outside their homes or on the sparse patches of suitable land that still remained on the Palestinian side of the wall.

As was the case with most of the village farmers, all of Abu Azzam's land ended up on the Israeli side of the wall. As he had done when his land was under threat for the creation of Zufin settlement, he resolved to resist, becoming head of the Land Defence Committee for the Qalqilya district. He also planted an additional 150 citrus trees to demonstrate his resolve to hold onto his land and as an insurance against confiscation under the Ottoman law. His son-in-law Abdul-Latif Khaled, equally dynamic and articulate, became the regional co-ordinator for the nationwide anti-apartheid wall campaign. Jayous became active in resisting the bulldozers: during one demonstration in December 2002, 100 locals and sympathisers from the International

Solidarity Movement were attacked by the IDF and Border Police and a number of protestors were injured. Non-violent protests continued throughout 2003 as the foundations for the wall were laid and five of the six agricultural roads that led to the village land were severed by the IDF. Soon, the area behind the levelled track was declared a closed military zone and private security guards prevented farmers from crossing to their fields. By summer 2003, ditches and razor wire had almost totally severed Jayous from its agricultural land. At night, local youths snipped the fence, and Border Police would enter the village, terrorising residents and shooting up water tanks.[46]

The villagers' anxiety was compounded by uncertainty. There were reports that a gate and permit regime would be introduced on completion of the wall but there was no official communication from the Israeli authorities regarding the operation of these crossing points or the criteria for obtaining the permits. Most farms in Jayous are small, family-based holdings that rely on high-intensive labour, especially during the olive harvest. In the long summer months, farmers prefer to work in the early morning and late afternoon when the heat is less intense. The produce of the greenhouses – tomatoes, cucumbers, beans and sweet peppers – requires daily irrigation otherwise these crops quickly fall victim to disease and rot. How would traditional ways and modern farming methods adapt to a regime that limited the number of farmers crossing and the amount of time they could spend in their fields? There was particular concern for the upcoming olive harvest – which accounts for the major part of Palestinian agricultural output – when men, women and children join together to collect the olives over the course of the six-week season.

By August 2003 the wall around Jayous was complete. Two gates were installed: a pedestrian gate for a Bedouin family whose house was isolated behind the wall and a crossing point for all the village farmers.[47] There was still no official word concerning the new access regulations so, fearful for their livelihoods, a number of farmers, including Abu Azzam, set up tents and temporary shelters beyond the wall. Their concerns were justified: for three weeks from late September the IDF closed the sole agricultural gate, preventing access to those who had not already camped out. Some 2,000 guava trees had to be harvested within 24 hours of ripening, and 80 per cent of the crop was ruined: in neighbouring Falamya 6,000 fruit and citrus trees perished. The farmers behind the wall were harassed by the army and their tents and shelters demolished. On the night of 14 October, the IDF rounded up most of the farmers and ejected them, with the warning that if they returned 'illegally' they would be fined and imprisoned.[48] Abu Azzam and other farmers managed to sneak back across the wall and hide out for several more weeks, before he left to recount his experience at the World Social Forum in Mumbai.

In mid-October villagers found new military orders pinned to rocks, proclaiming the areas behind the wall a closed area and announcing the new gate and permit regime. The villagers resolved not to apply for permits on principle: anticipating such a response, the Civil Administration delivered the permits to the municipality. As in Qalqilya City, allocation was haphazard: recipients included several residents long deceased, minors who did not require a permit according to the new regulations, and a Jayous resident who had emigrated to Australia 15 years before. More than 100 landowning farmers were refused permits, including 30 greenhouse owners. Abu Azzam was among those denied, as were many who had been active in the non-violent protests against the wall.[49]

Although the farmers had resolved not to apply, it was much more difficult to reject permits in hand, particularly as the olive season was imminent, and in the face of conflicting directives from the Palestinian Authority. Jayous farmers reluctantly submitted to the new regime, but once the initial three-month validity period expired, permits were not automatically renewed. Landowners were obliged to apply for extension to the Civil Administration, their lives becoming, in the words of B'Tselem, 'a bureaucratic nightmare' as they tried to meet the official requirements.[50] According to B'Tselem, as of March 2004 some 2,240 residents of Jayous and surrounding villages were granted permits while approximately 700 were rejected, a refusal rate of 25 per cent.[51] This assessment, however, is based on statistics supplied by the Civil Administration; most observers would put the percentage of refusals much higher as the figures do not include 'discouraged applicants' who have given up hope of receiving a permit. Most refusals were for 'security reasons', with no reason given and no entitlement to compensation for loss of income. However, refusals on security grounds were often reversed when those denied engaged Israeli attorneys or human rights organisations to support their appeals, suggesting that the security rationale for the original rejection was spurious.

An easing in restrictions towards the middle of 2004 may have come about due to pressure from ACRI. The Association submitted a petition to the High Court on behalf of Jayous and three neighbouring villages, charging that 'the gate opening times are severely limited, arbitrary and in no way reflect the basic needs of the population'.[52] At the court hearing, Chief Justice Aharon criticised the IDF: 'If you cannot provide solutions to the opening hours of the separation barrier [gates], then the barrier has to be moved'.[53] The state promised to increase the gate opening hours and accommodate them to the farmers' needs; although opening hours were indeed extended, they are still not convenient, especially for the many 'part-time' farmers who depend on farming to supplement their living. The late opening hours mean that the first tractors cannot return with that day's produce until late morning, so farmers have lost their traditional customers, the buyers who came directly to the fields in the early morning.

Local markets offer few alternatives in the depressed economy: the price of a 15-kilogram box of tomatoes declined from US$3.50 to less than 30 cents between March and July 2004. That autumn's olive harvest saw olive oil fall from US$5 to US$2 per kilogram, below the US$3 breakeven mark. With such returns, reinvestment in land is no longer feasible for many farmers, especially given the high costs involved in maintaining greenhouses. Abdul-Latif Khaled estimated that by August 2004, a year after the wall was completed around Jayous, local production had fallen from 7 to 4 million kilograms of fruit and vegetables, and that 15,000 trees had died. The number of farmers actively cultivating their land declined from 300 to 100, with over 170 farmers still denied permits.

In December 2004 the villagers discovered that bulldozers had arrived in the closed area behind the wall and were clearing away topsoil and uprooting olive trees in preparation for 'Nofei Zufin', an extension to Zufin settlement, that would include over 1,100 housing units.[54] The land in question is in dispute: the Israeli authorities claim it was sold to an Israeli company in the 1990s. Jayous residents contend that it was sold by subterfuge through a collaborator. New maps produced by the Civil Administration reveal different registration numbers and plans from the documents in the possession of landowners in Jayous. Part of Abu Azzam's land is included in the new confiscation plans, being now officially attached to the holdings of an émigré neighbour who did not join in the appeal against the first Zufin confiscation and consequently lost his land. Jayous secured a temporary injunction to halt the bulldozing, pending a judgement from the High Court. The

What does the wall mean?
By Abdul-Latif Khaled

I went to harvest some olives and I picked about 30 kilograms in two hours. The trees are full of fruits, but they wait for hands to carry them. The olives are fresh and shining, but wait for their people to visit them. The olive is a gift from God but now we cannot enjoy it.

As soon as I finished with the olives I went to pick some oranges, guava, tomatoes and cucumbers. I filled two boxes in ten minutes. I picked very fresh and tasty vegetables and fruits, but there is no market for them! I finished earlier than I expected because I was under stress for the gate to open and close.

I used the remaining time to have a look in the surrounding farms. In a neighbouring farm I saw what looks like a moaning under the trees. Most of the guava was on the ground and the floor was yellow. I've known the owner of the farm since I was a child. He used to come every day to take care of it. The trees are waiting for him to come and pick the fruits, but he does not come. When the fruits are ripe and are not picked, they fall immediately like tears, and you can hear the sound when they crash on the ground. So I understand why this man was crying when I met him two days ago. The Civil Administration refused to issue him a permit even though he is 65, although they had issued him one earlier this year.

When I went back I gave a box of guavas to him and I said 'It's from your land'. He said, 'I know that, thank you'. I asked myself, how can he know this? He answered, 'Myself I love, know and can feel my children even when I'm away from them'. His land must be like his children and they know each other, so that both are crying from being separated.

Do you know what the wall means? God knows and many friends also.

latest settlement expansion would not only result in another substantial loss of land but necessitate a long detour on the part of farmers to the land that remains. Additional confiscation orders in April 2005 – on this occasion affecting the little agricultural land left on the village side of the wall – were made for the purpose of building a road to link Jayous to the Falamya gate. Once this road is complete, the existing agricultural gate in Jayous will be shut and the farmers will have to travel an additional three kilometres each way to reach their land.

As a result of the circuitous route in the Jayous area, an area of some 27 square kilometres of fertile land lies between the wall and the Green Line, between the cities of Qalqilya and Tulkarm. Most consists of the cultivated farmland and orchards of Palestinian villages, now accessible to its owners, if at all, only by means of the gate and permit regime. That few Palestinians live on this land is no coincidence: for decades repeated requests by Jayous municipality to expand the residential area of the village westwards onto its extensive agricultural land have been turned down. This situation was institutionalised under the Oslo Accords when up to 60 per cent of the West Bank was designated Area C, and so remained under Israeli military and civilian control. Area C represents the few reserves remaining in which Palestinian communities can expand and build houses, but such construction requires Israeli authorisation. Between 1996 and 1999 only 79 such permits were granted,[55] leaving residents no choice but to build within already built-up Areas A and B. The alternative is to build 'illegally' in Area C and risk demolition.

The residential building that does exist within the 27 square kilometres belongs to the Jewish settlements of Zufin and Salit. These settlements are currently sparsely populated, but their master plans allow for growth far beyond their existing municipal boundaries. The present built-up area of Zufin covers 200 dunams, but 'the jurisdictional area of the settlement . . . encompasses an area that is ten times larger, some 2,000 dunams'.[56] Zufin holds 190 families but its website reveals future plans for 2,000 families, the 'natural growth' denied to the nearby Palestinian communities.[57] Hence, the December 2004 incursion onto land belonging to Jayous for the construction of Nofei Zufin.

Even allowing for natural growth and expansion onto contested land by the settlers, the majority of the 27 square kilometres still lies in the hands of its Palestinian owners. The landowners fear, however, that the same devices exploited to confiscate their land in the past will be employed again. Under the Ottoman system, the Sultan could take possession of *Miri* land – agricultural land situated close to places of settlement – if the farmer had not secured ownership by cultivating the land for ten consecutive years, or if the land had not been farmed at all for three consecutive years.[58] It is the latter provision which is causing most concern for Palestinian farmers. As a result of the low number of permit allocations and the limited gate opening hours, farmers are already cultivating their land infrequently, if at all, or opting for low-intensity, low-value crops. Those lucky enough to obtain permits also find it difficult to invest the time, labour and resources needed for long-term viability. Once this land is 'abandoned', they fear that the Israeli authorities will exploit the Ottoman Land Law and declare the areas concerned 'state land', to be utilised in the future for the expansion of the existing settlements and for the creation of new satellites.

More recent developments only serve to underline the farmers' fears. Whereas previously most members of an extended family could obtain a permit, since early 2005 eligibility has been increasingly restricted to the owners themselves, their spouses and their children. Nieces, nephews, uncles, cousins and grandchildren are no longer eligible to apply for permits, although the latter may do so upon presentation of a certificate of inheritance upon the grandparent's death. The reality is that most 'children' in this context are over 40 years of age and 'grandchildren' are generally young adults. These are the most able-bodied among the workforce, and the ones who most depend on the land for their present livelihood and for their future survival so that the younger generations can build houses and raise families. In addition, in certain areas in the northern West Bank, applicants who had previously received permits are now being rejected on the grounds that they do not own the land in question, despite their holding documents which were considered acceptable for the granting of permits in the past.[59] The full extent and the implications of these developments are not yet clear, but the suspicion is that the constraints resulting from the gate and permit regime are not just inevitable bureaucratic 'snafus' but a deliberate policy, 'the objective being to cause despair among the landowners in the hope that they will cease working their land in the seam area'.[60]

Like Mayor Zahran in Qalqilya, Abu Azzam also believes that economic strangulation and 'voluntary' emigration is the real purpose of the wall: 'they want the land without the people'. The livelihood and long-term viability of Jayous and its neighbouring villages depend on continued access to their land and water resources. Unlike the settlements, which are dormitory communities for the Tel Aviv area, the whole culture of the local Palestinian villages is tied up with the land, and their rhythm of life revolves around farming. It is for this reason that Abu Azzam is determined to keep cultivating his land whatever the cost. 'This land sent me to university, built my house, helped me raise my family. Without it we have no source of life.' However, even if the older generation of Palestinian farmers in the Green Line communities remains, what future is there

Haniya's story

In Bil'in in the Ramallah district, Haniya Hamada has been working her husband's family land since marrying into the village 50 years ago. A strong, confident and still cheerful woman in her late 60s, she counts the amount of her land not in dunams, but by the time it took her and her husband to plough with a horse: 13 days. On a normal day she goes to the land after early morning prayers and stays until midday, cultivating olives, wheat, barley and lentils according to the season. She and her husband raised and educated seven children on the proceeds of their smallholding, and she continues to work on the land by herself now that her husband is too old to toil and her children have all married and moved away.

Land levelling for the wall has begun, and already the bulldozers and the security guards are making it difficult to approach the land. Soon all that Haniya has carefully tended over the years will be lost, isolated beyond the wall along with the majority of Bil'in land. It is Friday, and Israeli and foreign activists are gathering in the village as they do after prayers every Friday to support local villagers in protesting the wall. In addition to the plastic bullets and the teargas, Bil'in has been used as a testing ground for all sorts of 'non-lethal' weapons: sponge and salt pellets and the 'screamer', a machine that emits a painful burst of high-pitched sound waves to disperse protestors.

Does Haniya have any hope that these demonstrations, with the participation of international and the Israeli activists, might succeed in altering the route? She smiles and looks doubtful and mentions with regret the hundreds of arrests and injuries over the previous months. None of this has had any effect on the route. In that case, does she have any expectation that she will be able to access her land once the gate and permit regime is introduced? She smiles and answers with a proverb:'Whoever catches a bird will never release it again.'

for their children who may not have the material resources or the determination to hold on to their inheritance? There are already indications of internal migration from affected areas, as evidenced by the several thousand residents of Qalqilya who have left since the wall was constructed. In Jayous too, many of the younger generation talk of leaving, believing they have no future in the shadow of the wall, joining the exodus of those emigrating or moving east to the central West Bank, 'the victims of strangulation by permit, intimidation and isolation'.[61]

NOTES

1. International Court of Justice, *Advisory Opinion*, para. 133.
2. Press conference by Israel, UN Headquarters New York, 9 July 2004.
3. World Bank, *Four Years – Intifada, Closures and Palestinian Economic Crisis: An Assessment*, October 2004, pp. xiii, xv – xvi.
4. The report noted that 'a glance at the map of West Bank food insecurity . . . suggests that food insecurity levels roughly match the path of the separation barrier.' Food and Agricultural Organization of the United Nations, *Food Security Assessment, West Bank and Gaza Strip: Main Report*, Rome, 2003, p. 38
5. UNRWA's *Food Security Survey: Localities Affected by Phase 1 of the Barrier* (unpublished) revealed that the wall 'is resulting in increased physical and economic obstacles to food security' in nine communities located in the 'Closed Zone'. The World Food Programme, had detected a 12 per cent rise in food insecurity in the Tulkarm district since 2003, 'attributable to the "Separation Wall" and the disruptions to the local economy with associated restrictions on movement of people, goods and services'. World Food Programme, *Support to the Palestinian Population Affected by the Conflict*, summer 2004, para. 11.
6. UNICEF, *Humanitarian Action: Occupied Palestinian Territory, Donor Update*, 10 November 2004.
7. Herb Keinon, 'Israel calls for ouster of UN food officer', *Jerusalem Post*, 14 October 2004.
8. HEPG/LACC, *The Impact of Israel's Separation Barrier on Affected West Bank Communities*, Annex III, April 2003, para. 14.

9. Abdel Rahman Al Tamimi, 'The wall's path is based on ultimate control over Palestinian water resources'; Khaled al Shanti, 'The apartheid cage around Qalqilya: Qalqilya's struggle for survival since 1948', in The Palestinian Environmental NGOs Network (PENGON), *The Wall in Palestine: Facts, Testimonies, Analysis and Call to Action*, June 2003, pp. 161–4, 175–8.

10. According to a World Bank survey conducted in 2001, 'the average time needed to bring products from the production site to an outlet within the West Bank and Gaza is three times longer now [than before the *intifada*]. The average distance to markets was approximately twice as long in June 2001 as it was a year earlier – 75 kilometers compared to 37 kilometers. . . . The average cost of transporting a truckload of produced goods has more than doubled, from approximately 170 NIS before the outbreak of the intifada to 370 NIS in June 2001. World Bank, *Fifteen Months – Intifada, Closures and Palestinian Economic Crisis: An Assessment*, March 2002, p. 7.

11. For a study of the changes in the application procedures for permits and the difficulties and costs involved in filing the application, see UNRWA, 'The permit system: the case of Jayous and Falamyeh', <http://www.un.org/unrwa/emergency/barrier/case_studies/permits.pdf> (accessed on 18 October 2005).

12. Marouf Zahran was defeated by a Hamas candidate in the municipal elections held in Qalqilya in May 2005. Hamas candidates won all 15 seats on the municipal council.

13. Gillerman had assured the Security Council that the wall 'does not annex territories to the State of Israel, nor does it change the status of the land, its ownership, or the legal status of the residents of these areas'. Statement of the Permanent Representative of Israel to the United Nations to the Security Council, 14 October 2003.

14. See UNRWA, 'Profile of the Alfei Menashe and Hable Enclaves', <Mhttp://www.un.org/unrwa/emergency/barrier/profiles/alfei.html> (accessed on 18 October 2005).

15. World Bank, *Four Years – Intifada, Closures and Palestinian Economic Crisis*, p. 49. UNRWA, the largest provider of educational services after the Palestinian Authority, was likewise forced to hire large numbers of extra teaching staff to cover teaching needs in remote areas. While this decentralisation mitigated the impact of closure to some extent, it also resulted in large numbers of teachers being forced to teach subjects outside their area of specialisation. UNRWA reported a dramatic decline

in exam pass rates between 2000/01 and 2003/04, especially in Arabic, mathematics and science. UNOCHA, *Occupied Palestinian Territory 2005: Consolidated Appeals Process* (Geneva, 2004), p. 20.

16. Drew Penland, 'A community rises up to stop construction of the apartheid wall', in Josie Sandercock et al. (eds), *Peace Under Fire: Israel/Palestine and the International Solidarity Movement*, (Verso, 2004), pp. 197–200.

17. The UN Special Rapporteur, John Dugard, made the following 'painful' observation at the Ras Atiya gate: '[I] saw young girls carefully searched by one soldier while another pointed a gun at her. Parents are not given permits to visit their children's school. (Would such a practice be tolerated by Israeli parents?)' *Question of the Violation of Human Rights in the Occupied Arab Territories, Including Palestine: Report of the Special Rapporteur of the Commission on Human Rights, John Dugard, on the situation of human rights in the Palestinian territories occupied by Israel since 1967*, 27 February 2004, para. 20.

18. 'When the wall is completed, up to 38,850 chronically-ill patients and 17,640 disabled patients may not be able to access essential specialized health care.' Medicins du Monde, *The Ultimate Barrier*, Jerusalem, February 2005, p. 15. As a result of the fragmentation of the West Bank and Gaza Strip by the closure, 'provision of essential reproductive health (RH) services for women has dropped from 82.4 per cent at the end of 2002 to 71 per cent at the end of 2003. The number of home deliveries is substantially higher in areas of the West Bank, which is heavily affected by internal closures.' UNOCHA, *Occupied Palestinian Territory 2005*, p. 11.

19. PENGON Anti-Apartheid Wall Campaign, 'Child unable to pass through the apartheid wall dies', 18 February 2004.

20. Health, Development, Information and Policy Institute, *Health and Segregation: The Impact of the Israeli Separation Wall on Access to Health Care Services*, 2004, p. 11. The survey also found that in affected communities in Qalqilya, patients have no access to ophthalmology, gynaecology, paediatric or dermatological services, with laboratory facilities, physiotherapy and services for diabetes patients severely limited, leading to 'a dramatic fragmentation of local health networks and referral systems'. Ibid., p. 10.

21. University of Geneva, Graduate Institute of Development Studies, *The Role of International and Local Aid during the Second Intifada: An Analysis of Palestinian Public Opinion in the West Bank and the Gaza*

Strip on their Living conditions, Report VII (Geneva, September 2004), p. 51. The survey also found that the percentage of respondents 'who needed hospitalisation and ambulance services, but were denied such services or obtained them after delay, was over twice that of respondents not living in areas crossed by the wall. The same disadvantage is apparent in reported access to educational services.' Ibid.

22. However, permits are not required for 'Israeli citizens and residents, including settlers living in the West Bank, or persons entitled to immigrate to Israel pursuant to the Law of Return, even if they are not Israeli citizens (i.e. Jews from elsewhere in the world)'. B'Tselem, 'Not all it seems', pp. 8–9. According to the UN Special Rapporteur, '[t]he prohibition on discrimination contained in many international conventions is clearly violated in the Closed Zone in which Palestinians, but not Israelis, are required to have permits', *Question of the Violation of Human Rights in the Occupied Arab Territories, including Palestine: Report of the Special Rapporteur of the Commission on Human Rights, John Dugard, on the situation of human rights in the Palestinian territories occupied by Israel since 1967*, Addendum 1, to the Sixtieth session of the Commission on Human Rights, 27 February 2004, para. 30.

23. See UNRWA, 'Profile: Barta'a Sharqiya enclave', <http://www.un.org/unrwa/emergency/barrier/profiles/bartaa.html> (accessed on 18 October 2005).

24. Amnesty International, *Israel and the Occupied Territories, Conflict, Occupation and Patriarchy: Women Carry the Burden*, March 2005, p. 4.

25. By March 2005, 627 Palestinian and 112 Israeli children had been killed in the conflict. *Question of the Violation of Human Rights in the Occupied Arab Territories, including Palestine: Report of the Special Rapporteur of the Commission on Human Rights, John Dugard, on the situation of human rights in the Palestinian territories occupied by Israel since 1967, to the Sixty-first session of the Commission on Human Rights*, 5 March 2005. para. 2.

26. Cairo Arafat, *A Psychosocial Assessment of Palestinian Children*, July 2003, pp. 5–6. <http://www.usaid.gov/wbg/reports/Final_CPSP_Assessment_English.pdf> (accessed on 18 October 2005).

27. The Palestinian Counseling Center, *The Psychological Implications of Israel's Separation Wall on Palestinians*, 13 January 2004.

28. ACRI Press Release, 'ACRI calls for dismantling of barrier in Alfei Menashe enclave', 5 September 2004. ACRI points out that 'there is no

partition or barrier between the villages of the enclave and Israel, which, it should be noted, directly contravenes the stated purpose of the barrier'. Ibid.

29. Save the Children UK and Save the Children Sweden, *Living behind Barriers: Palestinian Children Speak Out*, a paper presented to the UN Commission on Human Rights, March 2004, p. 11.

30. Amira Hass, 'Has the transfer of enclaves begun?' *Ha'aretz*, 24 February 2004.

31. B'Tselem, *Under the Guise of Security: Case Study: The Alfe Menashe Settlement*, <http://www.btselem.org/Download/200509_Guise_of_Security_Case_Study_Alfe_Menashe_Eng.doc> (accessed on 21 October 2005).

32. 'ACRI calls for dismantling of barrier in Alfei Menashe enclave.'

33. 'State to court: Palestinian villagers are pleased with the fence', *Ha'aretz*, 10 December 2004.

34. Dan Izenberg, 'Fence will destroy five villages', *Jerusalem Post*, 11 April 2005.

35. Ibid.

36. 'The High Court of Justice HCJ 7957/04 ruling on the fence surrounding Alfei Menashe', *Ha'aretz*, 15 September 2005.

37. Ibid.

38. Yuval Yoaz, 'Petitioners hail High Court's fence ruling as "very brave"', *Ha'aretz*, 15 September 2005.

39. Tovah Lazaroff, 'Alfei Menashe welcomes HCJ decision', *Jerusalem Post*, 16 September 2005.

40. Ibid. Since completion of the wall around Alfei Menashe, and in the belief that formal annexation would follow its *de facto* incorporation into Israel, housing prices in the settlement have risen by a third as Alfei Menashe 'has become a safer choice for people wanting to live over the Green Line and a more palatable option for those who want to live inside it'. Hilary Leila Krieger, 'Fence goes up – and so do prices', *Jerusalem Post*, 10 August 2005.

41. Hemi Shalev, 'Interview with Colin Powell', *Ma'ariv*, 1 August 2003.

42. B'Tselem, *Under the Guise of Security: Case Study: The Zufin Settlement*.

43. Palestine Hydrology Group, 'The impact of the wall's first phase on water', *The Wall in Palestine*, June 2003, p. 55.

44. B'Tselem, *Not Even a Drop: The Water Crisis in Palestinian Villages Without a Water Network*, July 2001, p. 4.

45. According to B'Tselem such appeals are futile: 'Past experience . . . indicate[s] that presenting objections to the IDF is nothing more than a formality which, in most cases, has no effect on decisions that have already been made.' *The Separation Barrier: Position Paper*, September 2002, p. 13.

46. A US journalist gave the following first-hand account: 'On August 4 [2003], this reporter was inside a home in the centre of the village, when the Border Police again entered at around sundown, dismounted from the jeep, and proceeded to shoot five [water] tanks in the area, including the one on the roof over our heads. After the police withdrew, water was streaming from holes in several of the tanks. . . . The next day the police came back, this time at 11 AM, and dismounted in front of the same house. The house's owner could hear two police talking as they stood directly outside, and methodically shot several more tanks. The houses normally have two tanks; the black ones are plastic, and hold cold water. The white ones are metal, and hold hot water. One officer said to the other, "shoot the white ones, they are harder to fix." His companion complied.' David Bloom, 'Palestinian farming village being strangled by wall', *World War 3 Report*, issue 95, February 2004.

47. In several locations in the northern West Bank, homes have been isolated in the closed area, cut off from their villages on the 'Palestinian side' of the wall. See UNRWA, 'Isolation of two refugee-owned houses in Ras village, Tulkarm', <http://www.un.org/unrwa/emergency/ barrier/case_ studies/jubara.pdf> (accessed on 18 October 2005).

48. Eight shepherds and 1,500 sheep were also evicted: with most of the agricultural land now beyond the wall, there is little grazing land left for these animals. See UNRWA, 'The grass is always greener on the other side of the fence: livelihoods at risk in Barta'a enclave and Jayous', <http://www.un.org/unrwa/emergency/barrier/case_studies/jayous-bartaa.pdf> (accessed on 18 October 2005).

49. Despite owning greenhouses he was rejected on the grounds that he only cultivated olive trees which, according to the Israeli authorities, require little care or cultivation. B'Tselem takes issue with this claim: 'The Civil Administration's assumption that olive groves require access to the orchards only during the olive-picking season is inaccurate. Cultivation of the orchards throughout the year, such as plowing, pruning, and weeding, greatly affect the yield and quality of the olives and the oil.' B'Tselem, 'Not all it seems', p. 10. Abu Azzam was eventually granted a permit, he believes, because of the negative publicity the refusal was

generating following his appearances at international meetings and solidarity events.

50. B'Tselem, 'Not all it seems', p. 12. The Association for Civil Rights in Israel (ACRI) also maintains that the permit 'system is arbitrary, and imposes an untenable burden of proof on the local population that turns their life into a bureaucratic nightmare'. ACRI Press Release, 'Permit allocation in enclaves severely violates basic rights', 25 January 2004.

51. B'Tselem, 'Not all it seems', p. 11.

52. ACRI Press Release, 'ACRI petitions Supreme Court: open access points in separation barrier', 29 December 2003.

53. ACRI Press Release, 'If you cannot provide solutions – the barrier must be moved', 4 May 2004.

54. The plan also included four nursery schools, an elementary school and a high school, several synagogues, a cemetery, recreation and sports facilities, and public open spaces. B'Tselem, *Under the Guise of Security: Case Study: The Zufin Settlement.*

55. B'Tselem, *Land Grab: Israel's Settlement Policy in the West Bank*, May 2002, p. 87. By contrast, with no impediments placed on settlement expansion under the Oslo Accords, the number of settlers in the West Bank and East Jerusalem rose from 247,000 to 375,000 between 1993 and 2001.

56. B'Tselem, *Under the Guise of Security: Case Study: The Zufin Settlement.*

57. The reporter, David Bloom, recounts that he and an Israeli activist from Jews Against the Occupation visited Zufin in August 2003 on the pretext of wishing to buy real estate and settle there. The estate agent took them on a tour and, pointing to Jayous's land, spoke of plans to build 1,000 housing units there. 'West Bank Apartheid: Israeli settlement expansion in Jayyous', *Znet*, 15 December 2004. <http://www.zmag.org/content/showarticle.cfm?ItemID=6875> (accessed on 21 October 2005).

58. 'Aerial photographs of the occupied territories enabled Israel to monitor the land use patterns of particular areas, and to ensure that any failure to cultivate was recorded and used against the owners.' Nicholas Guyatt, *The Absence of Peace: Understanding the Israeli-Palestinian Conflict*, Zed Books, 1998, p. 104. Israel, declaring itself inheritor of the powers of the Sultan, used these provisions to confiscate up to 25 per cent of West Bank land, primarily to establish Jewish settlements and to demarcate the master plans up to which these settlements could expand in the future. B'Tselem, *Land Grab*, pp. 52–54.

59. UNRWA/UNOCHA 'Crossing the barrier in the West Bank: Palestinian access to agricultural land', November 2005.

60. B'Tselem, 'Not all it seems', p. 12.

61. *Question of the Violation of Human Rights in the Occupied Arab Territories, including Palestine: Report of the Special Rapporteur of the Commission on Human Rights, John Dugard, on the situation of human rights in the Palestinian territories occupied by Israel since 1967,* Addendum 1, to the Sixtieth session of the Commission on Human Rights, 27 February 2004, para. 25.

Wall dividing the suburb of Abu Dis from Jerusalem

3 Enveloping Jerusalem

'MILITARY CONQUEST BY ARCHITECTURAL MEANS'

During the night of 31 July 2003, the Israeli Border Police descended on the village of Nu'man on the southern outskirts of Jerusalem. The police went from house to house in the Palestinian community – little more than a hamlet of 200 persons – and rounded up 19 of the males. Despite the show of force, and the fact that this was the third such incursion in as many months, security was not the main purpose of the operation. Instead, as Palestinians holding West Bank identity cards, the men were charged with illegal entry into Israel. Nu'man is situated inside the Jerusalem municipal borders, which Israel expanded and annexed after its conquest of East Jerusalem in 1967, and entry is forbidden to West Bank Palestinians without a special permit.

The men were taken into custody and released some hours later, having been warned of the consequences if they attempted illegal entry into Israel in the future. The men returned to Nu'man, so committing the offence for which they had been detained. Their recidivism was understandable: they were not 'illegal residents' in any normal definition of the term, such as Palestinians from the West Bank who had recently moved to Nu'man. On the contrary, they were returning to the village where they had been born and raised, a community founded in the 1930s before the creation of the state of Israel.

The absurd situation in which the residents of Nu'man found themselves dates back to the Six-Day War of June 1967 when Israel captured the West Bank, including East Jerusalem, which had been under Jordanian control since 1948. By the end of June the Israeli parliament, the Knesset, had approved the expansion of the existing municipal boundary to include not only the six square kilometres of Jordanian East Jerusalem but an additional 64 square kilometres encompassing 28 Palestinian villages in the surrounding hinterland. These 70 square kilometres were unilaterally and illegally annexed as sovereign territory to Israel; overnight Jerusalem became Israel's largest city in terms of size and population. The bulk of the territories conquered in 1967, the West Bank and Gaza Strip, were not formally annexed in the same way for fear of the consequences at the international level, and because there was no consensus within the Israeli establishment about their future status. Jerusalem, however, was considered of such political and symbolic value that annexation was worth the cost.

This *de facto* annexation was formalised in 1980 when the Knesset enacted the 'Basic Law', which stated that 'Jerusalem, complete and united, is the capital of Israel'. The international community has consistently and repeatedly rejected Israel's annexation of East Jerusalem through numerous Security Council resolutions affirming that all Israeli attempts to alter the character and status of East Jerusalem 'are null and void.'[1] Israel has shown characteristic disregard for such declarations and for international law, concentrating instead on creating geographic and demographic facts on the ground in order to establish exclusive Jewish hegemony over the city.

In addition to providing copious reserves of land for future Jewish settlement, the annexation brought some 70,000 Palestinians – residents of East Jerusalem and the surrounding villages – within the expanded municipal boundary. Following a census in 1967, these Palestinians were conferred not Israeli citizenship but permanent residency status. The blue Jerusalem ID cards granted their holders the right to live and move freely within Israel: by contrast, their West Bank and Gaza cousins, with orange or green ID cards, were adjusting to life under a military regime that continues to this day. For the succeeding decades, however, all Palestinians were able to travel and work inside Israel, as part of a policy of integrating the two economies, although only Jerusalem Palestinians were entitled to the same social, welfare and health benefits as Israeli citizens. On the other hand, unlike West Bank Palestinians, they had to pay a special municipal tax at the same level as their Jewish co-residents, while receiving few of the benefits. (The freedom of travel inside Israel ended after the Gulf War of 1991, when the state introduced a permit regime for West Bank and Gaza inhabitants wishing to enter Jerusalem.)

As West Jerusalem thrived and a settlement construction programme provided cheap and affordable Jewish housing throughout East Jerusalem and the annexed hinterland, the Arab neighbourhoods were ignored in terms of infrastructure and municipal services. Although the long-term mayor, Teddy Kollek, projected an image of benevolent concern for both parts of his unified city, his priorities in practice 'were the same as those of other Israeli leaders – to increase the Jewish presence in all parts of the city as fast as possible, while doing for the Arab residents only what was necessary to keep them placated'.[2] A 1991 report, suppressed because its findings were considered so damaging to Kollek, revealed that while Palestinians made up 28 percent of the city's population, they received only between 2 and 12 percent of the municipal budget.[3] Today, East Jerusalem continues to suffer from inadequate roads, lighting, sewerage systems and refuse collection, while being severely under-supplied with public parks, sports facilities and educational and cultural centres.

Interview with Mayor Teddy Kollek[4]

Kollek: We said things without meaning them, and we didn't carry them out. We said over and over that we would equalise the rights of the Arabs to the rights of the Jews in the city – empty talk. . . . Both Levi Eshkol and Menachem Begin [former prime ministers] also promised them equal rights – both violated their promise. . . . Never have we given them a feeling of being equal before the law. They were and remain second- and third-class citizens.

Question: And this is said by a mayor of Jerusalem who did so much for the city's Arabs, who built and paved roads and developed their quarters?

Kollek: Nonsense! Fairy tales! The mayor nurtured nothing and built nothing. For Jewish Jerusalem I did something in the past twenty-five years. For East Jerusalem? Nothing! What did I do? Nothing. Sidewalks? Nothing. Cultural institutions? Not one. Yes we installed a sewerage system for them and improved the water supply. Do you know why? Do you think it was for their good, for their welfare? Forget it! There were some cases of cholera there, and the Jews were afraid that they would catch it, so we installed sewerage and a water system against cholera . . .

These developments in urban Jerusalem had little impact on Nu'man, idyllically situated on the rural cusp of the Jerusalem and Bethlehem districts. The residents of the 27 other villages annexed when the Knesset extended the municipal boundary were granted the blue Jerusalem ID cards. The inhabitants of Nu'man, however, were mistakenly registered as residents of a nearby village outside the new boundary and thus received West Bank identity cards. As a result, an anomalous situation was created whereby the villagers were West Bank residents and subject to Israeli military rule, while their houses and surrounding land came under the Jerusalem legal and administrative system.

In the two decades succeeding the occupation this discrepancy went unnoticed. As long as the municipal boundary remained a line on a map, villagers could cross the notional divide between Jerusalem and Bethlehem, and between Israel and the West Bank. Indeed, residents claim that they were unaware that they were living outside the Jerusalem municipal boundary until informed by officials from the Ministry of Interior in 1992, and even then the consequence of their 'relocation' did not become evident. Life went on much as before, with villagers cultivating their olive trees and field crops on land which they owned or leased from landowners in nearby Bethlehem. They continued to tend their sheep as their Bedouin predecessors had done: residents still show visitors the cave where the founding patriarch and his extended clan, together with their flocks, used to winter. Nu'man benefited from the economic improvements of the 1970s and 1980s, the men working on construction sites in Israel and investing the proceeds to improve the existing houses and build more homes as their families increased. There were no schools or health services in the village, so parents continued to send their children to nearby Umm Tuba, now within the expanded municipal boundary of Jerusalem.

In other parts of unified Jerusalem substantial change was in progress. The Israeli-imposed municipal borders had been devised in such a way as to 'include the maximum territory possible, with the minimum possible Palestinian population'.[5] However, as the Palestinian birth rate was significantly higher than the Jewish one, it was decided to control, and if possible to curb, the Palestinian growth rate. This policy was formalised to maintain the 'demographic balance' in Jerusalem as it had stood at the end of 1972: 73.5 percent Jews to 26.5 percent Arabs. Two strategies were adopted. 'The first was rapidly to increase the Jewish population in East Jerusalem. The second was to hinder growth of the Arab population and to force Arab residents to make their homes elsewhere.'[6]

Israelis and Jews from around the world were encouraged to settle in Jerusalem and in the annexed hinterland, enticed by low or interest-free mortgages and by low-cost services.[7] To provide housing, and to forestall pressure for a withdrawal to the pre-1967 boundary, a large-scale settlement programme was undertaken in East Jerusalem and the surrounding area, primarily on private land expropriated from Palestinian owners. In the haste to assert political sovereignty and demographic dominance, municipal projects originally planned for other areas in Israel were implemented in Jerusalem 'irrespective of the topographical or social differences they were designed for'.[8] Over the years, twelve settlements were constructed, consuming more than a third of the 70 square kilometres expropriated from East Jerusalem and the West Bank: it was a policy of 'military conquest by architectural means'.[9] By the end of 2001, nearly 47,000 housing units had been built exclusively for Jews on this expropriated land but not a single one for Palestinians, although the Arab population in East Jerusalem had increased to some 230,000.[10]

The second principle – to hinder the numerical growth of Jerusalem Palestinians and encourage them to leave – was realised through the introduction of a range of discriminatory administrative measures. The expropriation of large swathes of land for Jewish settlement in itself substantially reduced the area available for Palestinian residential housing in East Jerusalem. More proactively, the authorities 'turned urban planning into a tool of the government' by secretly setting strict limits on the numbers of new homes that could be built in Palestinian neighbourhoods.[11] In 1974, the territory within the expanded municipal boundary was declared a regional planning area, and local councils were required to draw up local town planning schemes (TPSs), 'to define the development of the area, allocate territory in accordance with expected demand and population growth, and to determine infrastructure'.[12] In the absence of a TPS it was impossible to obtain a building permit, yet no planning schemes for Arab neighbourhoods were started until 1983 and by 1995 only seven had been approved.[13]

By contrast, in Jewish neighbourhoods, and especially in the settlements in the eastern part of the city, most planning schemes were granted after a maximum of three years. Here, the TPSs maximise population growth through the provision of a high proportion of houses and multi-storey buildings.[14] By contrast, the TPSs for Palestinian neighbourhoods ignore population growth, restricting the residential area allowed for housing in favour of civic buildings – which are rarely built, given the paucity of civic funding for Arab neighbourhoods – while only permitting construction in areas that are already built-up. In particular, little vertical building is allowed, on the grounds that 'small, low houses suit the rural character of the Palestinian neighbourhoods and the private building that prevails in them'.[15] A strict policy of demolition of houses constructed without the proper permits also reflects this discriminatory policy. Although 55 percent of building violations have occurred in West Jerusalem, 72 percent of house demolitions have taken place in East Jerusalem.[16]

The combined result of these restrictions was the migration of many East Jerusalem Palestinians to northern and eastern suburbs of the city outside the municipal boundary. Preferred areas were those close enough to allow for continued access to schools, health facilities and employment within official Jerusalem. A case in point is the A-Ram neighbourhood strategically located on the main Jerusalem–Ramallah road. A-Ram, which should have contained 20,000 residents by 2003 according to earlier census projections, had in reality swelled to between 50,000 and 60,000 by most estimates, with the 'migrants' making up 60 percent of the burgeoning population.[17] Jerusalem Palestinians who moved to areas such as A-Ram continued to pay their taxes and social security charges to the Israeli authorities and to receive social security benefits, thereby proving that municipal Jerusalem continued to be their 'centre of life' and retaining entitlement to their blue Jerusalem ID cards.

There was a further egregious method of restricting Palestinian growth, and one which would have implications for Nu'man. This was the designation of a large number of 'green areas' or open spaces, where building is prohibited, in the TPSs of Palestinian neighbourhoods. In theory, green areas are designed to safeguard the environmental character of a neighbourhood: in practice, the designation is 'intended to deprive the Palestinians of the right to build on their land, and to keep these areas in reserve for building earmarked for the Jewish population'.[18] For decades, Jabal Abu Ghneim, a forested hill next to Nu'man, was designated a green area, preventing its Palestinian owners from building on its slopes. In 1996, this same green area was bulldozed in preparation for the Jewish settlement of Har Homa, which would form a strategic link in a chain of settlements around the expanded municipal boundary. In addition, the creation of Har Homa impeded territorial contiguity between Palestinian villages in southern Jerusalem and the Bethlehem area. In the early 1990s, 5,000 dunams of land in and around Nu'man had also been designated a green area, prohibiting further construction within the village confines and signalling that its outlying lands – mainly belonging to residents of nearby Beit Sahour – might be expropriated for future settlement construction. Residents were left with no option but to build in any case, resulting in demolition orders being served on four of the village's 18 houses and, with the threat of demolition still in force, the owners were heavily fined for building 'illegally'. The fines do not nullify the demolition orders, and the injustice is all the more acute in that the settlement of Har Homa – illegal under international law – towers on nearby Jabal Abu Ghneim hilltop.

By now, tolerance of the village's anomalous status was coming to an end. The imposition in 1991 of restrictions on West Bank Palestinians entering Israel, including East Jerusalem – restrictions that were reinforced in 1993 – meant that residents technically needed permits to continue to reside in Nu'man. Repeated applications to be granted permanent status in Jerusalem were rejected on the grounds that the village had only been inhabited since the 1980s. This despite the fact that construction-dates from the 1950s are engraved on village houses and eleven homes are clearly visible in an aerial photograph from 1967 that the Israeli human rights group B'Tselem managed to obtain.[19] (The Israeli authorities claim that these houses were uninhabited or had been used by the Jordanian army.) In 1995, a letter arrived from the municipality prohibiting residents from sending their children to Umm Tuba, which pupils from Nu'man had been attending since the 1950s, since this school was reserved solely for residents of Jerusalem. Simultaneously, the municipality stopped providing water and sewerage services to the village. Fortunately, the Bethlehem municipality, now under Palestinian Authority control, filled this breach by providing basic services and allowing the children to attend schools in Bethlehem.

With the start of the second *intifada* in late 2000, the situation deteriorated further. The roads between Nu'man and Umm Tuba and Sur Baher were blocked by the IDF, further isolating the village from Jerusalem. Roads to the West Bank were also periodically blocked, and water and telephone services to Bethlehem were continually cut by the Jerusalem authorities on the grounds that the Bethlehem municipality had no business providing services inside Jerusalem. In 2003 the villagers learnt that the route of the wall would pass the village on its southern side. As no gates were planned, Nu'man would be physically separated from Bethlehem. Wall construction coincided with harassment by the Border Police, which residents believe was initiated to force them to leave the village. An anonymous individual accompanied by Border Police made frequent visits and, with a combination of threats (water supplies would be permanently cut off and the children unable to go to school in Bethlehem) and financial inducements (including compensation offered for houses built prior to 1992), insisted that they must leave. 'Otherwise,' he threatened, Nu'man would be cut off from both Jerusalem and Bethlehem, 'like a tree without water'. This individual was subsequently identified by *Ha'aretz* as a 'quasi-independent' contractor from the Ministry of Construction and Housing, employed to look for potential land for the creation of new settlements in East Jerusalem.[20]

A reprieve was gained when lawyers won a temporary injunction preventing the Border Police from arresting the residents for residing in Israel illegally. A further injunction has delayed completion of the wall in the area until the legal status of the village is resolved. Regarding their status, residents are prepared to accept either of two alternatives. If the wall route goes ahead as planned and severs them from the West Bank, they wish to have their presence within Jerusalem legalised by being granted the same permanent residency status as other Palestinians in the annexed areas. This would allow them to reside in Nu'man without fear of expulsion, and revive their former links to the southern Jerusalem villages of Sur Baher and Umm Tuba. Alternatively, should the Israeli authorities withhold the blue Jerusalem ID cards, they are requesting that the route be altered so that Nu'man is placed on the Bethlehem side of the wall, which has effectively constituted their centre of life for the last decade.

Given the adverse publicity that the Nu'man predicament is generating in the international media and from human rights groups, why have the Israeli authorities not decided on either option? The granting of Jerusalem ID cards to such a sparely populated village would have little impact, even for an authority obsessed with 'demographic balance'. The alternative of consigning Nu'man to the 'West Bank side' of the wall would not create a precedent: elsewhere, the route of the Jerusalem Envelope 'corrects' the expanded municipal boundary at several points, banishing unwanted high-density Palestinian population centres such as Shuafat refugee camp and Kufr Aqab to the West Bank side of the wall.

Evidently, the location of the village – located on 'a low hill that invites building'[21] – and its thousands of dunams of surrounding land, is deeply coveted by the Israeli authorities. A new bypass road linking Jewish settlements in the eastern Bethlehem district to Jerusalem via Har Homa is already under construction on village lands. In addition, more ambitious building plans for the lands of Nu'man exist: one of two major passenger and cargo terminals planned for the Jerusalem Envelope will be located nearby, and will require extensive land expropriation, the building of access roads and the construction of a Border Police station. The Jerusalem Municipality draft master plan foresees the expansion of Har Homa settlement eastward on the land and property of Nu'man.[22] More ambitious schemes envision the expansion of Har Homa much further to the east, connecting it with the large Maale Adumim settlement midway to Jericho through the creation of a chain of interlinking settlements.[23] Clearly, the realisation of these plans require extensive land expropriations, to which Nu'man presents an obstacle and its residents constitute a nuisance.

Should existing pressure fail to force the residents to leave Nu'man, there is another weapon in Israel's administrative arsenal that may yet tip the balance. The Absentee Property Law of 1950 was devised to expropriate the land and property of the hundreds of thousands of Palestinians who were expelled or fled during the 1948 Arab-Israeli war. Their assets were transferred to the 'Custodian of Absentee Property', which turned them over to the hundreds of thousands of Jewish immigrants who arrived in Israel in the early years of the state's creation. Although the Absentee Property Law has technically been applicable to East Jerusalem since 1967, the government decided that 'to have enforced this law would have been counter-productive both with regard to the Palestinian population and internationally, especially with the world's attention focussed on Israel's actions in the wake of the occupation'.[24] For some decades, West Bank Palestinians with land and property inside the expanded municipal boundary continued to have access to their assets, although many required permits to do so from the early 1990s.

By summer 2004, however, the completed southern section of the Jerusalem Envelope had 'absented' many West Bank Palestinians from their lands within the Jerusalem municipal area for more than a year, thus providing a new opportunity for expropriation. A cabinet meeting on 8 July gave the 'validity of a government decision' to a resolution passed the previous month by the Ministerial Committee for Jerusalem Affairs to apply the Absentee Property Law actively in Jerusalem. This decision meant that 'in the eyes of the government of Israel, these flesh-and-blood people, who live in Bethlehem or Beit Sahour or Ramallah and have olive groves or houses or land within the municipal boundaries of Jerusalem, do not exist. They are absentees.'[25]

As a corollary of the decision, the land concerned could be transferred to the Development Authority, a quasi-government body empowered to sell land for settlement construction. The amount of land and property involved was potentially enormous, and worth hundreds of millions of dollars. The decision was not made public and did not appear on the official government website that documents such actions, only coming to light through the efforts of Israeli attorney Danny Seidemann, a seasoned campaigner against administrative discrimination in Jerusalem. Seidemann had persistently petitioned the IDF to comply with its written assurances that it would grant access permits to his clients – Bethlehem farmers cut off from the lands by sections of the wall in the southern Jerusalem area. Eventually he received a letter from the IDF: 'The land no longer belongs to them, but is being placed in the possession of the Custodian of Absentee Property.'[26] In the face of international outrage and US displeasure the government rescinded the decision.[27] However, the Absentee Property Law has not been revoked; the decision has 'only killed the active use of the law for the time being', in Seidemann's words, and the law could be invoked at a more opportune time in the future.

The attraction of applying the Absentee Property Law to Nu'man is obvious. The land surrounding the village is for the most part carefully cultivated farmland, difficult to nominate as 'state land' – which had been the fate of much barren and rocky land in the West Bank. Most of it is the property of farmers from the Bethlehem area, whose access will be restricted following completion of the wall around Nu'man; it will then be easier to play on their 'absentee' status and invoke the law. Under the Absentee Property Law no appeal is possible and no compensation available, a further reason to employ the law in Jerusalem, where landowners have more legal redress than in the West Bank.

Confiscation of the surrounding land would leave the residents of Nu'man isolated on their little hilltop, while the expansion of Har Homa settlement, the construction of the terminal and the settlers' bypass road proceed on the expropriated land. Should they be unable to prove continuous physical presence in the village prior to its capture and annexation in 1967, and the Israeli authorities thus 'prove' that they are recent migrants from Bethlehem and therefore absentees in Jerusalem, their expulsion can also be expedited. In any case, denied entry into Jerusalem and cut off by the wall from Bethlehem, their basic services gone and livelihood threatened, there is little hope for the future. 'In these circumstances,' B'Tselem warns, 'it is likely that, sooner or later, the residents will be left no option but to leave the village'.[28]

THE JERUSALEM ENVELOPE: THE NEW MUNICIPAL BOUNDARY?

The wall marks the summation of Israel's policies in Jerusalem since 1967, literally setting in concrete the fruits of decades of annexation and settlement building. The route follows the expanded municipal boundary in the main – with the major exception of an enormous eastern detour to encircle Maale Adumim settlement – enclosing on the 'Israeli side' all the settlements constructed inside East Jerusalem and its annexed environs since 1967. The 1967 boundary was determined by political and strategic objectives without consideration for the fabric of life of the Palestinian population along its route. Communities linked by traditional social and familial ties found themselves arbitrarily assigned to one or the other side of a line on a map. Thus in the Sawahra area to the east of Jerusalem, West Sawahra and Jabal Mukaber were included inside the new municipal boundary while East Sawahra and Sheikh Sa'ad remained in the West Bank.[29] In practice, the Sawahra area is the home of one extended Bedouin clan scattered over many neighbouring villages. For much of the 1970s and 1980s the unilateral diktat dividing the communities made little difference to the residents' daily lives, with the Sawahra district developing into a contiguous suburban area on both sides of a notional line that was recognised neither by the locals nor by the international community.

The imposition of restrictions on entry into Israel after 1991 marked the beginning of a demarcation of jurisdiction and privilege based on residency status. Those on the West Bank side of Sawahra now required permits to cross the divide into municipal Jerusalem. This caused considerable bureaucratic and logistic difficulties for those holding West Bank ID cards: the secondary school, main health services and cemetery for Sheikh Sa'ad are located in Jabal Mukaber on the 'Jerusalem side' of the wall.[30] The restrictions were often absurd: to apply for a permit to enter the city legally, West Bank residents of Sheikh Sa'ad had to enter Jerusalem illegally in order to make the application. In practice, even without a permit it was possible to sneak across what remained an unmarked boundary, especially in times of low tension. The second *intifada* added checkpoints and physical obstructions to these administrative obstacles, physically delineating sections of the municipal dividing line for the first time since 1967. In September 2002, the IDF blocked the single road connecting Sheikh Sa'ad to Jerusalem, preventing all vehicular access, including the passage of ambulances. Those able-bodied and resourceful enough could still climb over the earth mounds and circumvent the Border Police patrols, in the process risking fines or imprisonment. However, the giant cement wall now cutting a circuitous swathe through the Sawahra area – and the A-Ram, Al-Azariya and Abu Dis neighbourhoods – will put an end to these traditional connections, severing families and isolating friends and neighbours from one another.

On completion of the wall, Palestinian residents of Jerusalem, whether holders of Jerusalem or West Bank ID cards, will face similar problems to those their cousins have wrestled with since the completion of the wall in the northern West Bank. Farmers will be cut off from agricultural lands, especially in the Ramallah and Bethlehem hinterlands, and in the Bir Nabala enclave where five villages will be enclosed. Access to health care, schools and workplaces, and to family and friends, will also be impeded, with consequences similar to those detailed in the previous chapter for Qalqilya. Access to Israeli health facilities will be a particular problem, given the higher standards of care available in Israeli hospitals, one of the principal reasons that Jerusalem Palestinians are anxious to retain their blue ID cards. Palestinian health-care provision will also be affected: many health facilities inside the municipal boundary serve the Palestinian community of the metropolitan Jerusalem area, including the Bethlehem and Ramallah districts. Indeed, many of the most specialised medical facilities are located inside municipal Jerusalem – and often represent the only such facility available in the West Bank and Gaza Strip. These include St John's Ophthalmic Hospital, Augusta Victoria Hospital – the only facility which provides specialist kidney dialysis, and the main referral hospital for refugees in the southern West Bank – and the Mukassad Hospital, which provides heart-care treatment. In turn, nearly 75 percent of the staff of the four main hospitals live outside the city.[31] These medical facilities also depend on West Bank patients for their economic survival, as do the many private schools which operate inside Jerusalem.[32]

In the rural northern West Bank, the gate and permit regime has already greatly restricted access and there is every indication that the largely urban Jerusalem area will suffer similar, if not greater, difficulties. Reports suggest that eleven transit points for vehicles and pedestrians, including two cargo terminals, are planned along the length of the Jerusalem Envelope. Although there has been no official announcement about the location and operational regime of these crossing points, access to some will reportedly be digitised by means of magnetic cards and will involve biometric identification in the form of a retina scan and fingerprinting. As many as 65,000 commuters could travel in each direction through these transit points daily, including Jerusalem Palestinian ID holders, West Bankers, Israeli citizens, settlers and the large number of expatriates and foreign employees of international organisations who work in the Jerusalem–Ramallah–Bethlehem triangle. It is unclear how the crossing points will cope with this passage of persons and goods, especially in the morning and afternoon rush hours: in A-Ram alone, an estimated 15,000 pupils commute to schools in East Jerusalem every day. There is little indication that the Israeli authorities have done any serious planning or allocated resources to deal with this enormous traffic of people and materials. On the contrary, concerned Israeli commentators have noted the 'glaring disparities between the declarations and intentions of senior security establishment officials and planners and the day-to-day reality'.[33] Although there have been promises to upgrade the 'level of service' and to reduce friction to a lower degree than what is currently encountered at checkpoints, the experience of Kalandia and Gilo checkpoints – the main northern and southern conduits into Jerusalem, where delays and shutdowns are routine – does not augur well.

The mechanics of daily crossing are an immediate worry, but a greater concern for Jerusalem ID holders is the possibility of losing their permanent resident status. The fear is that sooner or later the Israeli authorities will decree that the wall demarcates the new municipal boundary and cancel the Jerusalem ID cards of those residing on the West Bank side of the wall who cannot demonstrate that their 'centre of life' is within the new border or inside Israel proper. There is a precedent for this, as the Interior Ministry revoked the permanent residency status of thousands of Palestinians who had moved outside the Jerusalem municipal border between 1996 and 1999 on the grounds that permanent residency status, unlike citizenship, depends on the current domicile of the holder. More than 3,000 residency rights were revoked during the years of this 'quiet deportation policy' until the decision was reversed in 2000 and the residency of some of those affected was reinstated.[34] By then thousands of Jerusalem Palestinians who had been living outside the municipal boundary had 'returned' to Jerusalem for fear of losing their blue ID cards. In Danny Seidemann's words, 'this policy contributed more in improving the demographic statistics in favour of the Palestinians than all the maternity wards in East Jerusalem'.[35]

The 'centre of life' dilemma is most acute for areas such as Kfar Aqab and the Shuafat refugee camp, localities included in the expanded municipal boundary of 1967, but now banished to the West Bank by the route of the wall.[36] Some 30,000 Jerusalem ID card holders live in these areas; in total, an estimated 55,000 Jerusalem Palestinians may reside in localities that fall on the West Bank side of the wall. In addition, the situation of the unknown number of West Bank Palestinians residing illegally inside the current municipal boundary will become untenable, as will that of the thousands of 'mixed families' with spouses and children of different residency status. It can be assumed that the West Bank ID holder who remains on or moves to the Israeli side of the wall will run a greater risk of 'deportation' due to the increased security at the new crossing points.[37] Although the Israeli authorities have stated that the Jerusalem Envelope, like the wall in general, is a security measure and not a political border, this carries little weight in the face of such fears. The current municipal boundary was established by unilateral fiat and can be altered in the same way in the future, with no concern about the consequences for the Palestinians affected.

The phenomenon of Palestinians with Jerusalem ID cards migrating to within the municipal boundary – or to what is widely expected to be the new, wall-demarcated boundary – is one of the first, and unintended, consequences of the wall in Jerusalem: an estimated 1,000 out of 2,300 residents have already left Sheikh Sa'ad.[38] Much of the evidence to date is anecdotal: one report quoted 'a massive increase in the number of students' seeking to register for the 2004 school year in East Jerusalem.[39] At the same time, security officials reported 'a drop of tens of per cent in the number of children registered in kindergartens in Palestinian towns near Jerusalem', as their families moved to East Jerusalem.[40]

The most immediate impact is a housing shortage for these newcomers, particularly as restrictive building policies have severely limited available Palestinian housing. There is already evidence of a rise in real estate prices and rents in the relatively affluent Beit Hanina and Shuafat neighbourhoods in East Jerusalem.[41] Prospects for low-cost renting are less encouraging:

[129]

Shuafat refugee camp was one low-cost location in near proximity to the centre of the city, but is now cut off from Jerusalem by the route of the wall. One of the few alternatives remaining is the Old City of Jerusalem, but here the population density is already 10–20 times greater than in other parts of the city.[42] The lack of housing will be matched by a shortfall in physical and service infrastructure in the under-resourced Arab side: there is already a shortage of 1,300 classrooms for Palestinian children in East Jerusalem.[43] An indication that Israeli officials are belatedly recognising that existing services cannot cope with the influx is the decision to create a 'communal administration' to provide alternative services for those Jerusalem ID card holders living within the municipal areas that fall on the West Bank side of the wall. Deputy Prime Minister and ex-Mayor of Jerusalem Ehud Olmert was appointed by the cabinet to monitor the implementation of these emergency 'fabric of life' measures before the Jerusalem Envelope is sealed, leading one Israeli commentator to quip that this 'super-mayor' has to complete in 50 days, 'something that he did not do during his 10-plus years as mayor'.[44]

The increase in population density and occupancy rate and the resultant overcrowding are the first indicators of what many predict will be a decline in the living conditions of the Palestinian population on both sides of the Jerusalem Envelope. Commercial activity has already come to a halt in formerly vibrant business and shopping areas. In A-Ram, precast concrete sections of wall run down the middle of the main Jerusalem–Ramallah road, cutting off East Jerusalem customers from markets and retail outlets, and causing the owners of the defunct establishments to close up shop and join the exodus into municipal Jerusalem. Giant cement blocks eight metres high seal off other major suburban commercial centres such as Al-Azariya and Abu Dis, which as recently as 2001 enjoyed the

Interview with a resident of the Old City

I grew up in the Old City of Jerusalem, I have always lived there and I intend to die there. It's my community; I know everybody in my neighbourhood around the Via Dolorosa. I can get everything I need from the market and the shops; why do I need to live anywhere else? It is very crowded, however, and there are times I wish I could live somewhere with a bit more space for me and my family, with more rooms for the children and maybe a little garden. About eight years ago I bought some land in Abu Dis just outside Jerusalem. I had a little money at the time and the land was cheap – the person selling it needed money in a hurry, and I thought why not, maybe someday when I'm older and the children are grown up.

When they started building the wall, I knew that was the end of any hope of moving for me. I managed to sell the land in Abu Dis but for less money than I bought it for. It wasn't the end of the world. I was never really thinking of moving. But for my brother it was a disaster. He had made a lot of money and bought land in Semiramis, past Kalandia checkpoint near to Ramallah but still inside Jerusalem. He built a big house there for his family. When the *intifada* started and they made a border out of Kalandia checkpoint, he thought of moving. But he stayed. But then with the wall he had to move. So he's back now in the Old City. He's in one room in my house, our family house, he and his wife and four children. And I'm in another room with my wife and four children. Our mother has another room. He's renting his place in Semiramis and looking for land to buy inside Jerusalem, but where can you buy and what money would you need?

I know at least forty people who have moved back in our area. Most of the people who have shops in our neighbourhood live outside but now they are coming back and they're turning the shops into houses. There's not much business in the Old City anyway.

> The thing is I know I could sell our house for millions of dollars. You think I'm joking? It's a small place but it's on the Via Dolorosa and it's got a view of the Dome of the Rock and all the churches. Settlers, they come to me all the time. The last one said: 'here's my chequebook, here's my signature, you fill in the price you want.' But I will never sell.

lowest poverty rates in all the West Bank. As residents of these neighbourhoods lose their main customer base, Jerusalem Palestinians in turn are losing their access to the cheaper markets and labour and service resources on the West Bank side of the wall, leading to a significant downturn in the quality of life on both sides of the new divide.

In addition to the social and economic consequences, the likelihood is that the wall will create a new political reality and consciousness for Jerusalem Palestinians who have kept largely aloof from the national struggle, in general, and from the second *intifada*, in particular.[45] In Danny Seidemann's words, Jerusalem Palestinians 'have lived ambiguous lives, being "of" Palestine without being viscerally hostile to Israel'. The wall will put an end to this ambiguity and to the possibility 'in Jerusalem [of] a nonviolent equilibrium between Israelis and Palestinians'.[46] Seidemann is not alone among Israeli observers in warning of a radicalisation of East Jerusalem Palestinians as a result of the increased tension generated by the worsening of living conditions. In certain worst-case projections, this may lead to a 'Palestinisation' of the East Jerusalem population, resulting in 'a heightened sense of Palestinian national identity and [a view of] Jerusalem as the main arena for the national-religious struggle against Israeli rule (including violence and assistance to terrorists)'.[47]

Alarmed at the prospect of the wall causing a 'demographic boomerang' and political unrest, influential figures in the military and intelligence services, including National Security Advisor Giora Eiland, have recommended a radical re-routing of the wall to exclude most of the Palestinian neighbourhoods in East Jerusalem. However, faced with the prospect of re-dividing the 'unified city', the authorities balked. 'His [Eiland's] proposal was rebuffed, for political reasons. The government isn't ripe for that kind of decision yet, it was said.'[48]

Indeed, it was in connection with the wall around Jerusalem that the government conceded for the first time that there were political, and not just security, considerations in determining the route. In a petition to the High Court, the Council for Peace and Security – a left-leaning group of ex-military and intelligence personnel – had proposed an alternative route for the wall that would have re-divided the city on the basis of existing demographic realities, separating Jews from Arabs rather than 'unified Jerusalem' from the West Bank. Opposing the suggestion, the State Prosecutor argued that an alternative route which 'leaves the Arab residents of East Jerusalem on the other side of the fence also has political significance that cannot be ignored'.[49] It appears that once again political gain – in this case consolidating the expanded municipal boundary – trumped the security advantages of an alternative route that would have included fewer Palestinians on the Israeli side of the wall (assuming that such a structure is the best means to ensure security in Jerusalem).

Political and strategic considerations also underlie the plan to enclose Maale Adumim settlement by the wall – as approved by the cabinet in February 2005 – and thus extend the *de facto* borders of Jerusalem substantially eastwards towards Jericho, some 25 kilometres inside the West Bank. The decision coincided with the revival of the so-called 'E1' Plan – a scheme to fill in the area between Maale Adumim and East Jerusalem with a 'settlement corridor' of 3,500 housing units, industrial and commercial zones, and tourist resorts. Together the schemes would result in a chain of Jewish settlements surrounding and sealing off Arab East Jerusalem, eliminating the possibility of existing Palestinian communities expanding eastwards. Implementation of the E1 Plan would also sever territorial and transport contiguity between the northern and southern West Bank, effectively cutting the territory into two.

As East Jerusalem accounts for some 30 percent of Palestinian GDP, the Jerusalem wall combined with the E1 Plan would effectively destroy the geographical and economic viability of a future Palestinian state. Politically, in the words of the Palestinian Minister of State for Jerusalem Affairs, 'without Jerusalem as a shared capital for Palestinians and Israelis, there is no two-state solution'.[50] Indeed, Abu Mazen's inability to the counter the territorial and political onslaught on East Jerusalem 'has emerged as a critical issue used by domestic rivals to attack [him] and undermine the credibility of his methods and agenda'.[51] The wall around Jerusalem and the attendant E1 Plan, therefore represent 'a fact on the ground' that even the most accommodating of negotiators would find impossible to accept, let alone 'sell' to the Palestinian public.

The focus throughout this chapter has been on the consequences of the Jerusalem Envelope for the almost quarter of a million Palestinians who live within the expanded municipal boundaries. This is not to underestimate the significance of Jerusalem to the billions of adherents worldwide of the three global monotheistic religions. Hence the intention, under UN Resolution 181 of 1947, to partition Palestine into Arab and Jewish states but to place Jerusalem (and Bethlehem) under international supervision as a *Corpus Separatum*, with guarantees of freedom of access to the Christian, Jewish and Islamic holy places. In addition to restricting freedom of movement in general, the wall will further limit the ability of Palestinian Muslims and Christians to reach their mosques and churches, in violation of Israel's commitments under the International Covenant on Civil and Political Rights. The Al Aqsa Mosque and Dome of the Rock will be isolated within the fortified municipal boundary, becoming further off limits to Palestinian Moslems who already face age restrictions in travelling to the Haram Al Sharif for Friday prayers and religious festivals. The Church of the Holy Sepulchre and other Christian sites within the Old City will be similarly enclosed, and the traditional Good Friday and Palm Sunday processions obstructed by the wall through Al-Azariya. The wall will also totally sever the age-old link between Jerusalem and Bethlehem, in addition to cutting off Bethlehem from its agricultural hinterland. This will have implications in particular for the dwindling numbers of indigenous Palestinian Christians who live predominantly in the Bethlehem area, 10 per cent of whom have emigrated since the beginning of the second *intifada*.[52]

Concern for the future of Christian sites and for the viability of the Palestinian Christian community led to a rare letter of complaint to Prime Minister Sharon by a member of the US Congress, House International Relations Committee Chairman Henry Hyde, usually considered a staunch supporter of Israel. At the prompting of the Vatican, Hyde protested that the route of the wall 'will divide Bethlehem from Jerusalem, which threatens to stifle Christian life by preventing access to holy sites, places of prayer, and the contiguity of the Christian population'.[53] Similar concerns by the leaders of other Palestinian Christian denominations for their congregations – for example, the Bethlehem Lutheran Church – have led to the condemnation of the wall by churches worldwide.[54] Indeed, following the lead of the World Council of Churches, the wall has been a catalyst

Open Letter On The Status of Jerusalem[55]

From the World Council of Churches (WCC)

The World Council of Churches is deeply concerned about actions by the Government of Israel which threaten the achievement of a just peace for both Israel and Palestine by pre-empting negotiations on the final status of Jerusalem within the framework of international law. This letter reiterates the position of the WCC on a matter of critical importance.

While world attention is drawn to its Gaza withdrawal plans, the Government of Israel has intensified unilateral programs to consolidate control over Jerusalem and other occupied territory. These include:

- Creating a new *de facto* border by construction of the Wall on occupied territory, cutting all of annexed Jerusalem off from the West Bank in contravention of international law and the Advisory Opinion of the International Court of Justice in 2004.
- Cutting the West Bank in two by adding 3,500 housing units to Maale Adumim settlement. This decision mocks prospects for a viable, contiguous Palestinian State with a shared Jerusalem as its capital.
- Repeated declarations by the government's top leaders that large illegal West Bank settlements and all of Jerusalem will belong to Israel in any final agreement.
- Ongoing violations of human and civil rights of Palestinians in Jerusalem – illegal Jewish settlements are built in their neighbourhoods while construction permits for Palestinians are denied, family homes are demolished, requests for family reunification are denied.
- Threats and more threats, including an absentee property law allowing confiscation of Palestinian property in Jerusalem and a new regulation to require permits for Jerusalem residents entering the West Bank.

The WCC has long affirmed that the final status of Jerusalem must be part of a comprehensive peace settlement and be negotiated without delay; that the unilateral annexation of Jerusalem by the Government of Israel puts regional and world peace in jeopardy; that alterations of boundaries, population and settlements which change the religious, cultural or historical character of Jerusalem without the consent of the parties involved and the approval of the international community are violations of the Fourth Geneva Convention.

Irregular transfers of church-held land from one side to the other only add to the alarm of those who hope for justice; all such transfers must be annulled.

The WCC calls for an open and inclusive Jerusalem, a city of shared sovereignty and citizenship, a city of two peoples and three faiths, of Christians, Muslims and Jews. Now is the time to cease actions that pre-empt peace in Jerusalem and to begin negotiation of Jerusalem's final status within the framework of international law.

for many of the US branches of the global Protestant churches – Lutherans, Presbyterians, the Anglican Consultative Council, the United Church of Christ, Methodists – to call for divestment from companies who profit from Israel's occupation.

Despite these protests, the Israeli authorities appear determined on a route designed to consolidate Jewish hegemony over Jerusalem, to the detriment of Muslim and Christian Palestinians. However, as Danny Seidemann warns, 'public opinion – including in [the United States], in Europe and in Israel itself – will not tolerate the appropriation of Jerusalem in an exclusive way to the Jewish people'.[56] Changes in and to Jerusalem come under far more scrutiny than similar unilateral

Israeli measures elsewhere in the West Bank. In Seidemann's words: 'we can crush the people in Qalqilya to dust with impunity, and in a post-9/11 world the world will keep silent. But if we do that in Jerusalem it resonates.'[57]

NOTES

1. Security Council resolution 298 of September 1971 confirmed that 'all legislative and administrative actions taken by Israel to change the status of the City of Jerusalem, including expropriation of land and properties, transfer of populations and legislation aimed at the incorporation of the occupied section, are totally invalid and cannot change that status'. Following Israel's enactment of the Basic Law, the Security Council in resolution 478 of August 1980, further affirmed that 'all legislative and administrative measures and actions taken by Israel, the occupying Power, which have altered or purport to alter the character and status of the Holy City of Jerusalem . . . are null and void'. In its advisory opinion, the International Court of Justice also rejected Israel's claims to sovereignty over East Jerusalem, confirming that the West Bank and Gaza Strip had the status of 'occupied territories and Israel has continued to have the status of occupying Power'. International Court of Justice, *Advisory Opinion*, para. 78.

2. Amir S. Cheshin, Bill Hutman and Avi Melamed, *Separate and Unequal: The Inside Story of Israeli Rule in East Jerusalem* (Harvard University Press, 1999), p. 16.

3. Ibid., pp. 25–26. By 2002, Jerusalem Palestinians, 32 per cent of the population, were still receiving less than 12 per cent of the municipal budget. On average the Jerusalem municipality spends seven times as much on Jewish residents as on Palestinians, although the income of the former is approximately eight times that of the latter. Palestinian Academic Society for the Study of International Affairs (PASSIA), Jerusalem: Special Bulletin, June 2002.

4. Interview with *Ma'ariv*, 10 October 1990, quoted in B'Tselem, *A Policy of Discrimination: Land Expropriation, Planning and Building in East Jerusalem*, May 1995, p. 38.

5. Cheshin et al., *Separate and Unequal*, p. 37.

6. Ibid., p. 10.

7. Michael Dumper, *The Politics of Jerusalem since 1967* (Columbia University Press, 1997), p. 73. A proposal by Shimon Peres, then Acting Minister of Absorption, which was abandoned as too ambitious, recommended that 80 per cent of all new immigrants be directed to Jerusalem. Ibid., p. 286 footnote 66.

8. Ibid., pp. 111–112.

9. Ibid., p. 114.

10. B'Tselem, <http://www.btselem.org/english/Jerusalem/Discriminating_Policy.asp> (accessed on 18 October 2005). Of the 97,000 housing units built in Jerusalem between 1967 and the end of 2000, 82 per cent were built for Jews. Despite these efforts, by the end of 2003 the Palestinian population had grown by 225 per cent compared to a 135 per cent rise in the Jewish population, with the 'demographic balance' now standing at 67 per cent to 33 per cent. Apart from the much higher birth rate and younger population profile of the Palestinians, there has been an outflow of Jews, especially secular residents, from the city over the past decades. Etgar Lefkovits, 'Percentage of Jews in capital lowest since '67', *Jerusalem Post*, 2 September 2004.

11. Cheshin et al., *Separate and Unequal*, p. 31. This was only made public in 1993 following a City Council debate on the zoning plan for the Jerusalem Palestinian neighbourhood of Sur Baher. Seeking an explanation for restrictions in Sur Baher, Council member Sarah Kaminker woke up Mayor Teddy Kollek, who often dozed at council meetings. Kollek admitted that the policy had been in place since 1967. Ibid., p. 30.

12. B'Tselem, *A Policy of Discrimination*, p. 52.

13. Guyatt, *The Absence of Peace*, p. 143, footnote 23.

14. Ibid., pp. 129–131.

15. B'Tselem, *A Policy of Discrimination*, p. 60. B'Tselem contends that 'an examination of municipality documents shows that this is only a cloak for political considerations which are irrelevant to planning or sociological logic', pointing out that 'over the past 30 years, the Palestinians have undergone an urbanization process'. As an example of this discrimination, B'Tselem cites the contrasting plans for the Palestinian neighbourhood of Ras el-Amud and for a Jewish settlement in its midst. Plans for the former allow for a building percentage of 50 per cent of the allowable limit and two storeys while the latter permits 112 per cent and four storeys. In general, Palestinian areas are allocated percentages of 10–50 and two storeys, compared to up to 200 per cent and eight storeys in

Jewish settlements in East Jerusalem. Ibid., pp. 60, 61. B'Tselem concludes that the TPS for Palestinian neighbourhoods are 'not really town planning schemes at all, but "demarcation plans" . . . [whose] purpose is to grant legal validity to the prevention of building in most of the area of the Palestinian neighbourhoods'. Ibid., p. 58.

16. B'Tselem, <http://www.btselem.org/English/Jerusalem/> (accessed on 18 October 2005).

17. Robert Brooks, Rassem Khamaisi, Rami Nasrallah and Rana Abu Ghazaleh, *The Wall of Annexation and Expansion: its Impact on the Jerusalem Area*, The International Peace and Cooperation Center, Jerusalem 2005, p. 116.

18. B'Tselem, *A Policy of Discrimination*, pp. 58, 59. Kollek admitted the real reason for the policy when he disclosed to council member Sarah Kaminker, at a meeting of the municipality's finance committee, that an area on the edge of the Palestinian neighbourhood of Shuafat had been designated a green area 'to prevent Arab building [there] until the time was ripe to build a new Jewish neighbourhood'. Ibid., p. 59, footnote 161. As a result of the planning policy, Kaminker estimates that only 14 per cent of the entire area of East Jerusalem that was annexed to Israel in 1967 is earmarked for the development and building of Palestinian residential neighbourhoods. Ibid., p. 53.

19. B'Tselem, *Nu'man, East Jerusalem: Life under Threat of Expulsion, Status Report*, September 2003, p. 8. B'Tselem also obtained photos from 1977 and 1987 showing the growth of the village. 'This series of photos proves that Nu'man indeed existed prior to 1967 and that it gradually developed over time.' Ibid.

20. Uzi Benziman, 'The *hudna* came early', *Ha'aretz*, 19 June 2003.

21. Meron Rappaport, 'Land lords', *Ha'aretz*, 20 January 2005.

22. Ibid. 'Although the plan does not state explicitly that it will be a Jewish neighbourhood with several thousand units, it's obvious to everyone that this is the intention – the eastern continuation of Har Homa.'

23. Shahar Illan, 'Herzog's Greater Jerusalem', *Ha'aretz*, 16 February 2005.

24. Dumper, *The Politics of Jerusalem since 1967*, p. 43.

25. Rappaport, 'Land lords'. One of the two ministers responsible for the decision was Natan Sharansky whose book, *The Case for Democracy*, has been championed by President Bush and Secretary of State Condoleeza Rice as a catalyst for the spread of democracy through the Arab world.

26. Ibid. An accompanying letter from the office of the Custodian of Absentee

Property explained 'that their former owners, who are still registered as the owners of said properties, no longer hold any rights to them'.

27. The law was revoked on the urging of the Attorney-General, Menachem Mazuz, who claimed that the decision had been made without his knowledge or consent. However, four months after Mazuz's decision, the landowners concerned had still not received their permits and both the Ministry of Finance and the Ministry for Jerusalem Affairs maintained that his decision did not overrule the original cabinet decision. Meron Rappaport, 'Despite ruling by attorney general, Palestinians still denied access to their land, High Court petition charges', *Ha'aretz*, 11 May 2005.

28. B'Tselem, *Nu'man*, p. 24.

29. In practice the situation is more complex, as illustrated by the situation in Sheikh Sa'ad which is located in the West Bank. 'Fifteen houses situated in the northwest corner of the village lie within the jurisdiction of the Jerusalem Municipality. Seven other houses lie partially inside the city's border and partially in the West Bank.' B'Tselem, *Facing the Abyss: The Isolation of Sheikh Sa'ad Village – Before and After the Separation Barrier, Status Report*, February 2004, p. 5.

30. 'Crossing the valley on foot takes around forty-five minutes, and only individuals in good physical shape can negotiate the ascent.' B'Tselem, *Sheikh Sa'ad*, p. 5.

31. Rana Abu Ghazaleh, 'The torn Jerusalem fabric', in Brooks et al., *The Wall of Annexation and Expansion*, p. 84.

32. 'The municipality's investigation reveals that private schools in East Jerusalem are at risk of closure, because most of their teachers carry orange, Palestinian identity cards and live on the other side of the fence. A problem is also expected in state schools in the eastern part of the city because most of their teachers, who carry blue, Israeli identity cards, also live on the other side of the fence. Completion of the fence will make it difficult for them to get to work, and their chronic tardiness may affect the stability of the school system.' Jonathan Lis, 'A fence too far', *Ha'aretz*, 31 August 2005.

33. Michael and Ramon, *A Fence Around Jerusalem*, p. 89.

34. B'Tselem, <http://www.btselem.org/English/Jerusalem/Revocation_of_Residency.asp> (accessed on 18 October 2005).

35. Danny Seidemann, 'The separation barrier and the abuse of security', Foundation for Middle East Peace, <http://www.fmep.org/analysis/articles/separation_barrier.html> (accessed on 18 October 2005).

36. 'Why Israel chose to keep the refugee camp inside the city limits remains a riddle. One theory is that Israel never intended for the camp to remain but rather for residents to be sent elsewhere to live and the camp torn down to make way for Jewish development.' Cheshin et al., *Separate and Unequal*, p. 130.

37. See Gideon Levy, 'Twilight zone: partition plan', *Ha'aretz*, 3 March 2005, for an account of a couple with mixed Jerusalem and West Bank ID cards forced to separate because of the wall. 'The two girls will be under joint custody – three nights with dad, three nights with mom, and every other weekend with one of the parents.'

38. 'According to unofficial estimates, some 300 Palestinians with Israeli identity cards are returning to Jerusalem's municipal area every week.' Nadav Shragai, 'Palestinians left outside J'lem fence are moving into capital', *Ha'aretz*, 16 March 2004.

39. Yoav Stern, '3,000 Arab students will be forced to cross fence on way to school', *Ha'aretz*, 1 September 2004.

40. Amir Rappaport, 'Jerusalem is in demographic danger', *Ma'ariv*, 5 August 2004. This migration is ironic given that one of the major reasons for building the wall was to deter West Bank Palestinians from migrating to Israel for family and economic reasons. Approximately 250,000 Palestinian Arabs are thought to reside in Israel without permits, living mainly in Israeli Arab communities. 'Prime Minister Sharon said yesterday that once the separation fence is completed, the government will act vigorously to expel Palestinians living illegally within Israeli Arab communities . . . "Now it is a very difficult problem because of the absence of a fence. The minute the fence is closed, the activity to remove them will be much more vigorous, and their ability to return will be greatly reduced. Now when they are found and expelled, they come back."' Aluf Benn, 'We'll expel illegal Arabs from Israel', *Ha'aretz*, 2 April 2004.

41. Ironically, because of the high cost of housing in Beit Hanina and Shuafat, Palestinians are buying houses in the nearby settlements of Pisgat Zeev and Neveh Yaakov. 'Apartments in these Jewish neighborhoods are cheaper than in Arab neighborhoods, where prices have soared following the large inflow of Palestinians holding Israeli identity cards into the city.' Nadav Shragai, 'Study: separation wall negatively impacts J'lem residents and status', *Ha'aretz*, 6 October 2005.

42. Nadav Shragai, 'New J'lem master plan seeks to curb Old City overcrowding', *Ha'aretz*, 14 September 2004.

43. Sarah Kreimer, 'Testing democracy in Jerusalem', *Jerusalem Post*, 15 February 2005.

44. Meron Benvenisti, 'The disgrace outside their windows', *Ha'aretz*, 14 July 2005.

45. Although Jerusalem suffered more attacks, especially from suicide bombers, than any other Israeli city, with almost 300 killed and 2,000 wounded during the course of the *intifada*, the vast majority of the attacks were perpetrated by Palestinians from outside the city.

46. Daniel Seidemann, 'Why "separationism" won't work', *Ha'aretz*, 19 February 2005.

47. Michael and Ramon, *A Fence Around Jerusalem*, p. 106.

48. Nahum Barnea and Shimon Schiffer, 'Sticking to the Green Line', *Yedioth Ahronoth*, 29 July 2004.

49. Yuval Yoaz, 'High Court rejects petition against fence in Jerusalem', *Ha'aretz*, 22 June 2005.

50. Hind Khoury, 'Meanwhile, Israel grabs the rest of Jerusalem', *International Herald Tribune*, 11 August 2005.

51. The International Crisis Group, *The Jerusalem Powder Keg*, 2 August 2005, p.15.

52. Office for the Coordination of Humanitarian Affairs (OCHA)/Office of the Special Coordinator for the Peace Process in the Middle East (UNSCO), *Costs of Conflict: the Changing Face of Bethlehem*, December 2004, p. 18.

53. Akiva Eldar, 'People and politics: the Pope also wants a letter from Bush', *Ha'aretz*, 29 April 2004

54. Reuters, 'US Lutheran Church criticizes Israeli separation fence', 14 October 2005.

55. World Council of Churches, News Release, 31 March 2005, <http://www2.wcc-coe.org/pressreleasesen.nsf/index/pr-05-10.html> (accessed on 18 October 2005).

56. Seidemann, 'The separation barrier and the abuse of security'.

57. Ibid.

Wall and observation post near Aida refugee camp, Bethlehem, West Bank

4 The Wall and the International Community

THE WALL AND THE ROAD MAP

When Israel began construction of the wall in the second part of 2002 it attracted little international attention, coming as it did after the bloodiest period of the second *intifada*. Early 2002 witnessed a devastating round of suicide bombings inside Israel, including 29 fatalities at a Passover meal in the coastal town of Netanya in a single incident in March. This was followed by an IDF military offensive in the West Bank, which led to hundreds of Palestinian casualties, widespread destruction to Jenin and other cities, and the effective end of the Palestinian Authority as a governing entity. In the course of 2003, as the ambition and extent of the project was revealed, the wall was thrust onto the world stage. By the end of the year it was the subject of resolutions at the United Nations, with the General Assembly referring the question of the legal consequences of the route to the International Court of Justice (ICJ) for an advisory opinion.

By this time, the wall was also of interest to major external players, for it was being built against the background of an internationally sponsored peace process, the Road Map. Among the four sponsors of the Road Map (the 'Quartet'), the role of the Russian Federation was largely symbolic. The European Union, although a major player, appeared unwilling to assert its influence to a degree that reflected either its political and economic interests in the region or its stated positions on resolving the conflict. This left the stage to the other Quartet partners, the United States and United Nations, players with a long involvement in the Israeli-Palestinian conflict.

As the sole superpower and chief sponsor of the Road Map, the United States was the most influential external actor. Although purportedly an 'honest broker' between the two parties, the United States was also Israel's chief military, financial and diplomatic supporter. The Bush administration was regarded as the most sympathetic to Israel in US history, dominated by neoconservative hawks who regarded Prime Minister Sharon's Likud Party 'as the nearest thing they have to a sister party', in the words of a former British Foreign Minister.[1] Ideological sympathies were reflected in a mutual preference for unilateral action over multilateral consensus, and shared disdain for the constraints of international law. On the other hand, the United States had to demonstrate some degree of even-handedness to sceptical Arab and European allies and to engage more actively with the conflict in the political vacuum left after the IDF's military offensive.

Thus, in mid-2002, Bush's was the first administration to commit itself to the creation of a Palestinian state, albeit one with undefined borders and sovereignty, and which would only come about after the Palestinian Authority had instituted widespread reforms. It was uncertain how such a state would emerge given the opposition of Sharon, the main driving force behind the settlements and – once he had realised the strategic opportunities that the wall presented – the principal exponent of an annexationist route. It was also unclear how a route that annexed significant portions of West Bank territory to Israel was compatible with the 'independent, democratic and viable' Palestinian state that the Road Map was supposed to deliver.

US interest was muted during construction of the wall in the northern West Bank, but picked up in early 2003 with media reports of a settler-driven route that would intrude radically into the central and southern West Bank. In March, Abu Mazen was appointed the first Palestinian prime minister, a key Road Map provision; he was a person with whom the United States believed it could do business. The wall was now a crucial Palestinian concern, and the inaction of the Palestinian Authority was a serious grievance for the farmers affected by the levelling of land and uprooting of trees. Grassroots pressure was such that when National Security Advisor Condoleeza Rice visited the region in June, Abu Mazen complained that the wall was undermining 'the legitimisation of his government and the Palestinian public's faith in the [peace] process'.[2] Sensitive to any threat to Abu Mazen, Rice 'spoke out strongly against the project and urged changes' to the proposed route, especially to the large intrusion planned around the Ariel bloc of settlements.[3]

Sharon refused Rice's demands, but Abu Mazen had the opportunity to present his case directly to President Bush when he visited the White House the following month. He appeared to have succeeded: at their joint press conference after the meeting, Bush declared that it was 'very difficult to develop confidence between the Palestinians and Israel with a wall snaking through the West Bank'.[4] However, following his meeting with Sharon at the same venue a few days later, the president softened his position: 'the fence' had become a 'sensitive issue' rather than a 'problem'. Sharon was resolute and pledged to continue building the wall, while promising to make 'every effort to minimise the infringement on the daily life of the Palestinian population'.[5]

Sharon's concession reflected US concern at the prospect of the wall cutting off large numbers of Palestinians from their land and further undermining public confidence in Abu Mazen. The United States did not object to the wall in principle, nor to a route that contravened international law – as the ICJ advisory opinion would confirm – by running through the West Bank for most of its length. Washington also gave official, if qualified, endorsement to a route designed to bring the major settlement blocs onto the Israeli side of the wall: in April 2004, Bush would inform Sharon by letter that the United States accepted that these 'major Jewish population centres' would accrue to Israel following final status peace talks. Such annexation should be by agreement between the parties, however, unlikely though it was that a credible Palestinian leader would emerge to agree to such concessions. In the meantime, a solution had to be found that would not prejudge final status outcomes or provoke undue humanitarian and political discontent. The main issue was still the planned route around the Ariel bloc of settlements, which would encompass a huge swathe of West Bank territory and affect dozens of rural villages in the Qalqilya and Salfit districts.

In the 'breach plan' the two sides found a compromise that squared the circle of US concerns and Sharon's strategic objectives. Individual barriers would be erected around the Ariel bloc settlements, but these would not be linked together or connected to the main wall until an unspecified future date. This satisfied the United States that the main route did not stray too radically, or with too much negative humanitarian impact, into the West Bank, while the temporary barriers would not represent a permanent or irreversible 'fact on the ground' for future negotiations. For his part, Sharon had secured agreement that the Ariel bloc would be enclosed within the main wall in the future and that the overall route enjoyed US blessing. Moreover, the United States did not object to the route in the

Jerusalem, Ramallah and Bethlehem areas, which brought large strategic settlements and land reserves for future expansion onto the 'Israeli side' of the wall. The only major settlement cluster left outside was the Maale Adumim bloc, located between East Jerusalem and Jericho, whose inclusion within the main route would raise humanitarian and political issues as problematic as those of Ariel. A gap was left in the route at this critical point to be closed at a more opportune moment.

It was only when he had received the all-important US imprimatur that Sharon brought the route before the cabinet for approval in October 2003, where it was passed by a large majority. The Quartet partners were dismayed by the cabinet decision: the first official map released to accompany the decision demonstrated – if proof was still needed – the true annexationist purpose of the wall. UN Secretary-General Kofi Annan warned that settlements and the wall represented 'serious obstacles to the achievement of a two-State solution'. EU foreign policy chief Javier Solana called on Israel to respect international law and 'put an end to the building of the separation wall that invades territories far beyond the 1967 lines'.[6] For Sharon the concerns of the Quartet were irrelevant; the route had been worked out bilaterally with the United States in talks between Sharon's bureau chief, Dov Weisglass and National Security Advisor Condoleeza Rice.[7] Secretary of State Colin Powell was largely excluded from these deliberations, being considered less sympathetic than other administration officials to Israeli concerns. It was Powell who proposed penalising Israel by deducting the cost of the intrusive route in the West Bank from $US 9 billion in loan guarantees the US Congress had approved for Israel, a threat that was publicly brandished and then quietly dropped the following year.[8]

The Palestinian Authority had no influence over the debate on the route: 'We are not very engaged or even consulted on those discussions', complained an adviser. 'Again we have a situation where Israelis and Americans are making decisions that Palestinians are going to have to pay for.' Palestinian marginalisation had increased with the resignation of Abu Mazen in September 2003. While he had been Prime Minister and the wall viewed as a threat to his legitimacy, the United States was prepared to exert some influence on Israel. With his demise, a principle reason for US leverage on the wall was removed, and the United States now appeared to accept 'not only the idea of the fence, but also its deep penetration into the West Bank'.[9]

Alarmed by the cabinet-approved route, the Palestinians turned to the United Nations. On 14 October, the Arab League requested a special meeting of the Security Council at which they submitted a draft resolution declaring that construction of the wall beyond the Green Line was contrary to international law and must be ceased and reversed. Italy, speaking on behalf of the European Union, expressed strong opposition to the route in the West Bank and urged Israel to respect the principles of international law. However, when it came to the vote, the United Kingdom and Germany – two EU countries on the 15-member Council – abstained. In any case, the United States used its veto power as a permanent member of the Council to kill the resolution. Expressing what was by now the standard Washington position, the US representative John Negroponte made no reference to international law, declaring only that the wall should not intrude on the lives of Palestinians or prejudge the outcome of final negotiations. Negroponte was still insisting that the Road Map was the way forward, to which the PLO representative, Nasser El Kidwa, replied: 'You cannot have construction of the expansionist wall and simultaneously pretend that the Road Map exists. It's either/or.'[10]

Thwarted by the US veto, the Arab League requested a resumed emergency session of the General Assembly 'in light of the inability of the Security Council to fulfil its responsibility for the maintenance of international peace and security due to the exercise of one of the permanent members of the veto'. The procedure was based on the 'Uniting for Peace' resolution of 1950, an initiative designed to circumvent automatic Soviet vetoes in the Security Council by referring issues to the General Assembly. Unlike the Security Council members, no member of the 191-nation General Assembly wields a power of veto, but for all its significance in representing the will of the international community a General Assembly resolution is non-binding. A draft resolution was circulated, essentially the same as that vetoed by the United States the previous week. In an unexpected move, a second draft text was introduced seeking an advisory opinion from the International Court of Justice as to whether Israel was legally obliged to stop construction and dismantle the wall. However, following negotiations between the European Union and Arab governments, the text requesting the advisory opinion was dropped.

On 21 October Italy, on behalf of the European Union, introduced a revised draft resolution expressing the General Assembly's concern that the route of the wall could prejudice future negotiations, make the two-state solution impossible and cause further hardship to the Palestinians. The resolution demanded that Israel 'stop and reverse the construction of the wall in the Occupied Palestinian Territory, including in and around East Jerusalem, which is in departure of the Armistice Line of 1949 and is in contradiction to relevant provisions of international law'. It also requested that the UN Secretary-General submit a first report on compliance within one month, following which further actions could be considered within the UN system.[11] All the EU countries were among the 144 who voted in favour, while the United States was one of the four who voted against.

Despite this resounding international censure, Israel vowed to continue construction. Unsurprisingly, the Secretary-General's report the following month found that Israel was not complying with the resolution. Another emergency session of the General Assembly was convened at which the PLO proceeded to reintroduce the draft resolution requesting an advisory opinion from the International Court of Justice on the legal implications of the route through the West Bank and East Jerusalem. The European Union again pressed to have the text withdrawn. Failing this, the EU countries abstained in the 8 December vote, on the basis of 'the conviction of many Member States that transferring the matter of the Wall to a legal forum would do nothing to advance the political process necessary for peace'.[12] Despite this, the resolution was passed, with 90 in favour, eight against and 74 abstentions.

The Secretary-General's report had noted that 'in the midst of the road map process the Barrier's construction in the West Bank cannot, in this regard, be seen as anything but a deeply counterproductive act'.[13] It was ironic therefore, that only a few weeks previously, the Security Council had formally endorsed the Road Map in Resolution 1515, in the face of vehement Israeli objections. In effect, the Map was moribund, although the sponsors would continue to go through the motions as if the plan still constituted the basis for a viable peace process. Soon Sharon would announce its successor, the Disengagement Plan, and move to get the United States on board. First however, the sides were preparing for the contest at The Hague, where the legal consequences arising from the route of the Wall through the West Bank and East Jerusalem would be examined.

THE WALL AND THE INTERNATIONAL COURT OF JUSTICE

The International Court of Justice was set up after the Second World War to resolve international disputes and to issue judgments in cases where the states concerned agree to accept its decision. In a case such as the wall, where one party refuses to accept its jurisdiction, the ICJ is authorised to deliver a non-binding legal opinion if requested by 'duly authorised international organs and agencies' such as the UN General Assembly. Israel made much of the fact that the ruling would be non-binding – meaning that the Court could not enforce its judgement – and insisted that this diminished its importance. However, as the Association for Civil Rights in Israel pointed out, the ICJ 'is the most senior judicial tribunal that is authorised to interpret and determine what constitutes international law, and therefore the contents of the advisory opinion are binding'.[14] The ruling which the ICJ delivered, therefore, would have authoritative status in international law.

Nor would the Court be pronouncing on the wall *in vacuo*: the General Assembly resolution explicitly requested that the ICJ render its advisory opinion 'considering the rules and principles of international law, including the Fourth Geneva Convention of 1949, and relevant Security Council and General Assembly resolutions'. Israel's flouting of UN resolutions was well known, but it was also in opposition to the majority of world opinion with regard to international law in general, and the Fourth Geneva Convention specifically. The Fourth Geneva Convention of 1949 and the Hague Regulations of 1907 set out the rules that apply to the conduct of states during wars and occupations, and provide for the protection of civilians. Although Israel has ratified both the Hague Regulations and the Fourth Geneva Convention, it argues that the latter is not applicable to the West Bank and the Gaza Strip *de jure* since neither was the territory of a High Contracting Party to the Convention when captured by Israel in 1967. However, Israel claims to apply the humanitarian provisions of the Convention *de facto*, without specifying which of the provisions it considers 'humanitarian' and what this application entails in practice. Rejecting Israel's position, the other High Contracting Parties to the Convention, the International Committee of the Red Cross – the promoter and guardian of international humanitarian law – the UN Security Council and General Assembly, have repeatedly reiterated that the Fourth Geneva Convention applies *de jure* in the occupied territories.

In practice, Israel has employed self-serving interpretations of the two legal instruments for an expansionist agenda rather than for the benefit of the population under occupation – 'protected persons' under the Fourth Geneva Convention. Both the Convention and the Hague Regulations prohibit the occupying power from expropriating private land unless absolutely necessary for military purposes. In the first decade after 1967, Israel made extensive use of a provision that allows the requisition of land and buildings for a temporary period to house military forces and support units.[15] However, the majority of the land expropriated was used not for military purposes but to establish civilian settlements which, far from being temporary, continue to expand three decades later. The settlements themselves are in violation of both the Hague Regulations, which forbid permanent changes to occupied territory that do not benefit the local inhabitants, and the Fourth Geneva Convention, which prohibits an occupying power from transferring members of its own population into occupied territory.[16]

In succeeding decades selective interpretations of the same articles were used to justify more extensive land confiscation. The Hague Regulations require an occupying power to respect the laws applying in an occupied territory, but permit the power to manage these areas and to derive profits therefrom. Israel used provisions from the Ottoman Land Law, incorporated into the Jordanian legal system, to confiscate up to 40 per cent of West Bank land, again primarily for establishing Jewish settlements. Although the land is taken for exclusive Jewish use,

Israel claimed that 'the establishment of the settlements is a lawful act of deriving profits which, in addition, contributes to maintaining the properties of the Jordanian government'.[17] Given Israel's history of violating international law, its unease at the upcoming proceedings was understandable. It was not only the invasive route that would come under international legal scrutiny, but also the settlements the wall was designed to annex, as well as Israel's status as an occupying power, and the applicability of the Fourth Geneva Convention and other key instruments of international law to the occupied territories.

Anticipating that it would lose the legal argument, the Israeli establishment was divided over the proper strategy to adopt towards the upcoming proceedings. Some recommended boycotting the Court altogether, to undermine the international legitimacy of the case. Others maintained that since the hearing would be held regardless of whether Israel attended or not, a snub would give the Palestinians free rein at an important international forum. There was concern in Israel at the efforts that the Palestinian Authority, which had hitherto shown little leadership in addressing the wall, was investing in the upcoming campaign. Within the cabinet, Justice Minister Tommy Lapid was foremost among those arguing that Israel must present its case. However, aware that the cabinet-approved route of October 2003 was indefensible, Lapid proposed abandoning the sections that intruded most deeply into the West Bank, so shortening the route by 200 kilometres. The alternative, he warned, was Israel facing 'international boycotts as was South Africa before the fall of the regime'.[18] The proposal was rejected, as were three similar proposals for a shorter route submitted by opposition party Knesset members.

However, Sharon was himself moving for alterations to the route, involving tactical, 'humanitarian' changes. By his own admission, although the wall had been successful in preventing suicide attacks it was 'unsatisfactory in the harm it does to Palestinians' daily lives'.[19] He was aware of Israel's vulnerability on the humanitarian issue: a member of the US Congress had recently complained to him of watching Palestinian children climbing over the wall: 'How will Israel contend with these severe things?' the congressman demanded to know.[20] How indeed, for the testimony of those isolated by the wall in enclaves and closed areas would have a high profile in the Palestinian strategy at The Hague. It would take more than the cosmetic changes already implemented to offset such damaging images: the 'security fence' had become the 'anti-terror fence' on the advice of French public relations consultants. Another suggestion was to paint the concrete sections of the wall 'so that it will be more aesthetic and the public relations damage will be reduced'.[21]

Sharon's proposed changes were also prompted by the acting Attorney General, who admitted that she would find it difficult to defend sections of the existing route before the Israeli High Court. The High Court had agreed to bring forward a hearing of two petitions by Israeli rights groups on behalf of Palestinian villagers concerning the legality of the wall within the West Bank and of the gate and permit regime, as a 'dress rehearsal' for the ICJ proceedings. In the High Court case the state's attorney confirmed the government's intention of making changes to the completed route, bringing portions of the projected route closer to the Green Line and of changing the permit regime.[22] As part of this flurry of activity to blunt criticism on the humanitarian front, a Defence Ministry task force requested the addition of 'hundreds of millions of shekels to the budget' to ease life in the closed areas, to bus children to schools, and to construct dozens of alternative roads, tunnels and gates.[23] On the day before the ICJ hearings commenced, the IDF, with the international media in tow, dismantled an eight-kilometre section that had isolated the Palestinian town of Baqa Sharqiya within a closed area. Plans to build the Jordan Valley wall were also quietly dropped, 'because of the diplomatic damage [Israel] is likely to endure as a result'.[24]

In addition to Dov Weisglass's shuttling to Washington to coordinate the positions of the two governments, the Israeli authorities also enlisted the support of Jewish organisations in the United States. In a campaign of letter writing, newspaper op-ed pieces and talk-show call-ins, the argument was repeated that the inconvenience caused by the 'anti-terror fence' was temporary and reversible, whereas death by terrorism was permanent. It was not the fence that should be on trial but terror itself. This blitz undoubtedly had an effect: an opinion poll in late January showed that support for the wall in the United States had risen to 47 per cent, although the finding that 'Republican men of moderate education' were its strongest supporters may have tempered enthusiasm slightly.[25] There was also a campaign by prominent supporters of Israel to delegitimise the ICJ itself, and the expected critical opinion, with celebrity lawyer Alan Dershowitz smearing the ICJ as 'a kangaroo court'.[26] Prominent members of Congress such as Hillary Clinton were vocal in their opposition to the proceedings. John Kerry, the frontrunner in the race for the Democratic Party presidential nomination, had reversed his earlier opposition and was now describing the wall as 'a legitimate act of self defence'.[27] Israel, officially through its foreign ministry and through friends in Congress, was also pressing the United States to delay publication of the State Department's annual report on human rights around the world, fearing that the expected harsh criticism of the wall and the humanitarian suffering it inflicted would be used against it at The Hague.[28]

After hearing the advice of its legal team, the cabinet decided that Israel would not attend the oral hearings, lest its appearance lend legitimacy to the case. However, a 120-page written affidavit was submitted to the ICJ, arguing that the Court had no authority to pronounce on what was a political rather than a legal matter. Israel's defence for building the wall was woven into this procedural argument: the wall was its legitimate way of exercising its fundamental right to self-defence, and the dramatic decline in suicide attacks since its partial completion vindicated this. Israel also appealed to the countries that had voiced reservations or abstained in the General Assembly resolution to question the jurisdiction of the ICJ in their written submissions and to boycott the oral hearings.

That the United States in its submission stated that the ICJ was not the proper forum for what was a political dispute came as no surprise, nor did its decision to shun the oral proceedings.[29] However, Israel considered the European Union's written submission and its decision not to attend the hearings a major triumph. The European Union's written submission, a letter from the Irish Presidency, accepted that that route of the wall through the West Bank was illegal, but viewed an advisory opinion as inappropriate since it would not help the two parties to re-launch a political dialogue. At a debate in the European Parliament concerning the wall, a member pointed to 'the inconsistency of our position of urging [Palestinians] to give up violence, while simultaneously denying them the chance to seek redress through international legal institutions'.[30] This inconsistency was reflected in the national submissions tended by individual EU member states, with the United Kingdom and Germany arguing that the Court should decline to render an advisory opinion, and Sweden and Ireland raising no objection to the Court's examination of the issue.

One of the most widely anticipated hearings in the Court's 57-year history began on 23 February 2004. Almost 50 countries had volunteered written submissions but only 13 states, including Palestine, and two organisations – the Arab League and Organization of the Islamic Conference – participated in the oral hearings. There was satisfaction on the Israeli side that only Arab and Moslem states or organisations were appearing, together with South Africa, Cuba, Belize and Madagascar – 'the usual collection of dictatorships and Arab states against Israel' – and that all of the 'enlightened' western democracies had declined to attend.[31] Despite Israel's refusal to appear before the World Court, the court of world public opinion was considered too important to be left to the Palestinians and a huge public relations exercise was organised 'to make the Palestinians regret the day they ever sent the matter to the court'.[32] A hearing was organised in parallel to the official proceedings, a 'public trial of terror', in which Israeli victims recounted their experience and suffering. The Jewish Agency organised a solidarity march in which 927 protestors held placards with the names of all the Israeli fatalities of the second *intifada*. The skeleton of a bus blown up in Jerusalem the previous month in which eleven people were killed was prominently displayed.

Palestinian demonstrations were more muted, despite the fact that, as one Israeli commentator noted, they 'could easily pull out photographs of more than 3,000 victims. But instead of harping on their misfortunes, they have focused on Israel's occupation policies and the security fence. They have appealed to the world's sense of justice, while we seek the world's pity.'[33] Palestinians were encouraged in the lead-up to the hearings by the publication of reports by respected international organisations, which were unanimous in concluding that the existing and proposed route of the wall violated both international humanitarian law and international human rights law.[34] In addition, the International Committee of the Red Cross had taken the unusual step of issuing a public statement expressing concern about the humanitarian impact of the wall and warning that, 'in as far as its route deviates from the "Green Line" into occupied territory [it] is contrary to International Humanitarian Law'.[35]

The ICJ advisory opinion was not delivered until July and was much more powerful than most had anticipated, with the sole dissenting voice on certain issues that of the US judge, Justice Buergenthal. Rejecting the contention that the question of the wall was outside the Court's jurisdiction, the justices ruled that the ICJ had the authority to give an advisory opinion and could find 'no compelling reason for it to use its discretionary power' not to do so'.[36] The judges also rejected Israel's argument that a situation of armed conflict existed in the territories and that military necessity justified the wall, instead finding that 'the infringements resulting from that route cannot be justified by military exigencies or by the requirements of national security or public order'.[37] They also rejected another key Israeli contention, that the main treaties and instruments that make up international human rights law were not applicable to the West Bank and Gaza. Rejecting Israel's position, the ICJ found that both international humanitarian law and international human rights law were applicable to the occupied territories, and that by impeding the liberty of movement of Palestinians and their rights to work, health, education and an adequate standard of living, the wall violated international human rights law.[38]

The ICJ also rejected the long-standing Israeli claim that the West Bank and Gaza Strip are not occupied territories and that the Fourth Geneva Convention is not applicable. To the contrary, the Court affirmed that 'all these territories (including East Jerusalem) remain occupied territories and Israel has continued to have the status of occupying Power', and that 'the Convention is applicable in the Palestinian territories'.[39] It therefore followed that all settlements, including those in East Jerusalem, 'have been established in breach of international law'.[40] As 'the route chosen for the wall gives expression *in loco* to the illegal measures taken by Israel with regard to Jerusalem and the settlements', the ICJ found that the wall and its associated gate and permit regime contravene the Fourth Geneva Convention.[41] The Court also found that, despite Israel's claim that the structure was temporary, the wall creates 'a *fait accompli* on the ground that could well become permanent, in which case . . . it would be tantamount to *de facto* annexation'.[42] In all, the ICJ was unequivocal: 'The wall, along the route chosen, and its associated régime gravely infringe a number of rights of Palestinians residing in the territory occupied by Israel. . . . The construction of such a wall accordingly constitutes breaches by Israel of various of its obligations under the applicable international humanitarian law and human rights instruments. . . . The Court accordingly finds that the construction of the wall, and its associated régime, are contrary to international law'.[43]

Having demonstrated the wall's illegality, the Court ruled that Israel 'is under an obligation to cease forthwith the works of construction of the wall . . . including in and around East Jerusalem, to dismantle forthwith the structure therein situated, and to repeal or render ineffective forthwith all legislative and regulatory acts relating thereto'.[44] Israel is also under an obligation 'to make reparations' for the 'requisition and destructions of homes, businesses and agricultural holdings' and 'to return the land, orchards, olive groves, and other immovable property seized'.[45] Nor did legal obligations rest with Israel alone: 'all States are under an obligation not to recognize the illegal situation resulting from the construction of the wall [and] are also under an obligation not to render aid or assistance in maintaining the situation created by such construction.'[46]

Reactions to the advisory opinion were predictable. Officially, Israel vocally rejected the ruling – 'this resolution will find its place in the garbage can of history', according to Ra'anan Gissin, senior advisor to Sharon[47] – and promised to continue construction. However, the wider implications of the ruling, particularly concerning Israel's status as an occupying power and the illegality of the settlements, caused widespread dismay – not least among the Israeli legal establishment – both from the point of view of Israel's standing in the international community and from concerns about the possibility of punitive action. A week before the ICJ advisory opinion the Israeli High Court, in examining the planned route of the wall in the Ramallah area, had ruled that as a general principle, there should be a proper balance between security and humanitarian considerations. Sharon adopted the High Court recommendations, which had accepted the State's argument that the route was determined by security rather than political considerations and could be built in the West Bank, as a means of taking the sting out of the ICJ advisory opinion.

Palestinians were jubilant at the Court's vindication of their position, and vocal in asserting that the advisory opinion should pave the way for a campaign of concerted international action against the wall and settlements, in the same way that a 1970 ICJ advisory opinion condemning South Africa's illegal presence in Namibia had been instrumental in leading to sanctions against the apartheid regime. The European Union gave a cautious response, noting that the advisory opinion 'will need to be studied carefully'. There was no such restraint in the United States, with public figures condemning the verdict and the House of Representatives passing a resolution by an overwhelming majority, deploring the UN General Assembly's 'misuse' of the ICJ.[48] The Arab League quickly moved to introduce a draft resolution in the General Assembly demanding that Israel comply with the ICJ advisory opinion. Predictably, the United States voted against Resolution ES-10/15, but there was shock in Israel that the European Union countries voted *en masse* with the 150 majority member states in favour.

However, far from being a foretaste of international reaction to come, the ICJ advisory opinion and General Assembly Resolution ES-10/15 marked the high point of international action. Although the advisory opinion represented an unequivocal condemnation of the wall and settlements, and of Israel's violation of international law, there was no will to enforce the decision, and the clause regarding the international community's responsibility to ensure compliance by Israel went unheeded. By the time the advisory opinion was delivered in July 2004, Sharon's disengagement plan was in full flight and the international community, preferring the allure of political progress offered by the plan to the hard choices involved in persuading Israel to implement the advisory opinion, was enthusiastically on board.

UNILATERAL DISENGAGEMENT: GAZA FOR THE WEST BANK

The basic principles of the unilateral disengagement plan were set out in a speech Sharon delivered at a conference in Herzliya in December 2003, warning that if the Palestinians 'still continue to disregard their part in implementing the Roadmap', Israel would soon have no alternative but to 'initiate the unilateral step of disengagement from [them]'. The plan was 'unilateral' in the sense that Sharon denied the need for a Palestinian partner. In practice it was bilateral, with the United States enshrined as the sole outside adjudicator: at the Herzliya conference, Sharon stressed that the 'unilateral steps will be fully coordinated with the United States'. The attraction of this arrangement was that it entailed negotiating with an administration sympathetic to Israel rather than with the Palestinians. Israeli-US negotiations also avoided the constraints and balances that multilateral bodies such as the European Union or United Nations could bring to bear, while totally sidelining international law.

All the parties concerned, including Israel, were initially at pains to insist that the Road Map was still on course: the European Union cautiously welcomed disengagement only as the first step in implementation of the Road Map.[49] In practice, disengagement meant abandonment of the Road Map and whatever slight influence the other Quartet members had been able to exert on the political process. Disengagement also put paid to alternatives, such as the Geneva Initiative, which were attracting increasing attention internationally as the Road Map faltered. With disengagement Sharon came up with a plan driven by his own strategic vision: as Dov Weisglass, one of the principal architects of disengagement, explained, 'it compels the world to deal with our idea, with the scenario we wrote'.[50]

The disengagement plan entailed the removal of all the Jewish settlements in the Gaza Strip and four isolated settlements in the West Bank, accounting for fewer than 10,000 of more than 400,000 settlers in the occupied territories, including East Jerusalem. Much was made of the fact that Sharon, the main architect of the settlement enterprise, should be the first Israeli Prime minister to uproot settlements in the occupied territories. However, Sharon was not a sudden convert to the principles of international law or the binding nature of Security Council resolutions. The reasons for the Gaza withdrawal were demographic: the number of Jewish settlers in the Gaza Strip had never attained a demographically critical mass, and Gaza was viewed by most Israelis as outside the 'national consensus'. In practice, Sharon was giving up untenable settlements in Gaza and the northern West Bank the better to consolidate Israel's hold of more strategic areas of the West Bank and to expand

Manoeuvre of the century

Interview with Dov Weisglass[51]

Ha'aretz: I want to remind you that there will also be a withdrawal in the West Bank.

Weisglass: The withdrawal in Samaria is a token one. We agreed to only so it wouldn't be said that we concluded [only fulfilled] our obligation in Gaza.

Ha'aretz: You gave up the Gaza Strip in order to save the West Bank? Is the Gaza disengagement meant to allow Israel to continue controlling the majority of the West Bank?

Weisglass: Arik [Sharon] doesn't see Gaza today as an area of national interest. He does see Judea and Samaria [the West Bank] as an area of national interest. He thinks rightly that we are still very, very far from the time when we will be able to reach final-status settlements in Judea and Samaria.

Ha'aretz: Does the evacuation of the settlements in Gaza strengthen the settlements in the West Bank or weaken them?

Weisglass: It doesn't hurt the isolated, remote settlements; it's not relevant for them. Their future will be determined in many years. When we reach a final settlement. It's not certain that each and every one of them will be able to go on existing.

On the other hand, in regard to the large settlement blocs, thanks to the disengagement plan, we have in our hands a first-ever American statement that they will be part of Israel. In years to come, perhaps decades, when negotiations will be held between Israel and the Palestinians, the master of the world will pound on the table and say: We stated already ten years ago that the large blocs are part of Israel.

[165]

Ha'aretz: Is he sacrificing a few of his children in order to ensure that the others remain permanently where they are?

Weisglass: At the moment he is not sacrificing anyone in Judea and Samaria. Until the land is quiet and until negotiations begin, nothing is happening. And the intention is to fight for every single place. That struggle can be conducted from a far more convenient point of departure. Because in regard to the isolated settlements there is an American commitment stating that we are not dealing with them at the moment, while for the large blocs there is genuine political insurance. There is an American commitment such as never existed before, with regard to 190,000 settlers.

Ha'aretz: So you have carried out the manoeuvre of the century? And all of it with authority and permission?

Weisglass: When you say 'manoeuvre', it doesn't sound nice. It sounds like you said one thing and something else came out. But that's the whole point. After all, what have I been shouting for the past year? That I found a device, in cooperation with the management of the world, to ensure that there will be no stopwatch here. That there will be no timetable to implement the settlers' nightmare. I have postponed that nightmare indefinitely. Because what I effectively agreed to with the Americans was that part of the settlements would not be dealt with at all, and the rest will not be dealt with until the Palestinians turn into Finns. That is the significance of what we did. The significance is the freezing of the political process. And when you freeze that process you prevent the establishment of a

> Palestinian state and you prevent a discussion about the refugees, the borders and Jerusalem. Effectively, this whole package that is called the Palestinian state, with all that it entails, has been removed from our agenda indefinitely. And all this with authority and permission. All with a presidential blessing and the ratification of both houses of Congress. What more could have been anticipated? What more could have been given to the settlers?

them. Significantly, in the year prior to the disengagement the number of settlers in the West Bank increased by 12,800, even allowing for the evacuation of the four northern settlements.[52]

This was hardly a hidden agenda: at Herzliya Sharon declared that, within the framework of the plan, Israel 'will strengthen its control over those same areas in the land of Israel which will constitute an inseparable part of the State of Israel in any future agreement'. Dov Weisglass was even more explicit, explaining that the removal of the four settlements in the northern West Bank was 'a token one', agreed to 'only so it wouldn't be said that we [only fulfilled] our obligation in Gaza'. In return for the evacuation of 10,000 settlers through the disengagement plan, and perhaps another 10,000 from the West Bank at some stage in the future, 'Sharon can tell the leaders of the settlers [that] he is strengthening the other 200,000, strengthening their hold on the soil'.[53] That many settlers were too ideologically blinkered to appreciate the trade off was unfortunate. Instead of demonstrating against the plan, Weisglass admonished them, 'they should have danced around and around the Prime Minister's Office'.[54]

Instead of dancing for joy, the settlers' YESHA Council came out strongly against the principle of uprooting Jews from any part of the land held by Israel. However, Sharon's domestic travails did him no harm diplomatically, rallying international support that grew increasingly enthusiastic when it became clear that he was serious about pushing through with his disengagement plan despite strong domestic opposition. Political dividends arrived as early as April 2004 in the form of a letter from President Bush. 'In light of new realities on the ground, including already existing major Israeli population centers', Bush wrote, 'it is unrealistic to expect that the outcome of final status negotiations will be a full and complete return to the armistice lines of 1949'.[55] The Bush letter was widely interpreted as signifying that the United States would endorse Israel's annexation of the large settlement blocs following a comprehensive peace agreement, with the qualification that such annexation would be 'mutually agreed' between the parties. For Sharon, such negotiations were far in the future, and in the long interim period more 'facts on the ground' could be created within the blocs to ensure their eventual annexation to Israel.

Throughout the summer of 2004 Sharon accelerated building in the settlements, despite a public promise to the United States to limit such construction and the Road Map's obligation of a complete freeze on all such activity. For all the standard protestations from the United States, according to the *New York Times*, the Bush administration had 'signalled that it would accept housing growth within the boundaries of existing settlements', to lend political support for Sharon in 'a difficult political spot' due to tensions within his own Likud party over disengagement.[56] The central role of the wall in drawing the new border around the 'inseparable parts' of the West Bank was clear: 'Israel will greatly accelerate construction of the security fence', Sharon had announced at the Herzliya conference. The ICJ proceedings were an unwelcome irritant but the tactical changes made to the route in response to international criticism did not significantly affect the strategic gains. However, a revision of the cabinet-approved route of October 2003 was necessary in light of these alterations and the new guidelines arising from the Israeli High Court's rulings.

A revised route was not brought before the cabinet for approval until February 2005 but negotiations with the United States on the adjustments began almost a year before. The United States agreed that the October 2003 route would remain as a 'vision', but 'problematic areas . . . which stirred U.S. criticism will either not be built at present, or will be constructed in a manner that minimizes inconvenience to Palestinians who live in nearby villages'.[57] Plans to construct inner barriers that would have fenced in tens of thousands of Palestinians in the Salfit and Ramallah areas were dropped, not least because visiting US experts had dismissed Israeli claims that the barriers were necessary to protect Ben-Gurion airport from missile attack.[58] The most significant change to the route itself was in the southern Hebron area, where the wall was brought significantly closer to the Green Line. As a results of these changes, the amount of land annexed *de facto* between the wall and the Green Line declined from over 16 to 10.1 per cent, and the numbers of Palestinians on the Israeli side of the wall dropped significantly from 189,000 to 49,000. However, despite the ICJ advisory opinion calling for the dismantling of those sections of the wall already constructed, and an end to the gate and permit regime, there were no significant changes to the wall in the northern West Bank, which the international community appears to accept as yet another Israeli fait accompli.

With inconvenience to Palestinians resolved, at least to the satisfaction of Sharon and the United States, that still left the 'problematic areas . . . which stirred US criticism'. Specifically, there was Ariel and its adjoining settlements, whose inclusion within the main wall route would seriously impair the territorial contiguity needed for a future Palestinian state. On the other hand, Ariel was one of the principal settlement blocs that Bush in his April 2004 letter had agreed Israel would eventually annex. The solution was the old 'breach plan': temporary barriers would be constructed around the main settlements in the 'Ariel Finger' but these would not be joined together or linked to the main wall route for the present. This solution allowed the United States to maintain that these structures were temporary and did not preclude 'future diplomatic options', while Sharon could claim that this temporary arrangement would become permanent in the fullness of time.

The result – for all the tweaking of the Green Line and the significant reduction in the number of Palestinians in closed areas and enclaves – was a wall that allowed Sharon to keep the major settlement blocs: Ariel, those in the Greater Jerusalem area and the Etzion bloc in Bethlehem. There was also a significant addition: the Maale Adumim bloc, located between Jerusalem and Jericho, was included on the Israeli side of the wall in the route brought before the cabinet for approval in February 2005. Maale Adumim, the largest settlement in the West Bank, had not been included in previous plans because of expected US disapproval. As with Ariel to the north, the route around Maale Adumim would serve as a 'contiguity breaker' between the central and southern West Bank, while also sealing off Arab East Jerusalem from the rest of Palestine.

Although the planners' revised proposal incorporating these changes was approved by Sharon and Defence Minister Shaul Mofaz in September 2004, Sharon bided his time before bringing the complete revised package before the cabinet for approval. In his eyes, the addition of Maale Adumim was more than generous compensation for the few isolated settlements lost by the re-routing of the wall in the Hebron area. However, he was concerned that these losses would be used as 'ammunition by Jewish settlers already enraged at his disengagement initiative'.[59] On the other hand, the inclusion of Maale Adumim was expected to arouse international disapproval. The solution was to bring both the disengagement plan and the revised route for approval at the same cabinet session, 'in an effort to neutralize criticism of the fence route by coupling it with the decision to evacuate settlements'.[60] The revised route was passed by a large majority in the Israeli cabinet, which now included members of the Labour Party as coalition partners. Sharon was correct in anticipating muted international criticism. Typical was the reaction of the United Kingdom, whose ambassador to Tel Aviv, while delivering an official protest at the inclusion of Maale Adumim and its satellite settlements within the revised route, admitted that the protest 'wasn't a great big production number, because the same cabinet also took the key decision on implementing disengagement'.[61]

By now, the disengagement plan was the only game in town and the international community which had viewed Sharon 'as a scary and war-mongering bully, is now petting him and embracing him, tenderly covering him up so he won't catch a chill', the Israeli political commentator Aluf Benn observed, 'the main thing being that he remain prime minister and evacuate the Jewish settlers from the Gaza Strip and the northern West Bank in the near future'.[62] By August 2005, as the attention of the international community was focused on the disengagement operation in the Gaza Strip, all pretence by Sharon of adhering to the 'breach plan' – temporary barriers for the Ariel and Maale Adumim settlement blocs – was gone. 'The Ariel bloc will remain a part of Israel forever, connected territorially to Israel', he promised, while 'Ma'ale Adumim will continue to grow and be connected to Jerusalem'.[63] Typically, Sharon waited until the disengagement operation was in full flight before handing out expropriation orders to Palestinian landowners for the wall around the Maale Adumim settlement bloc.[64] At the same time, as a first step in the inauguration of the controversial E1 Plan for building in the terrain between Maale Adumim and East Jerusalem, Sharon expedited the construction of a police headquarters and access roads in the area, despite earlier US objections.[65]

Disengagement blindness on the part of the international community was all the more remarkable in that Sharon's *de facto* annexation of strategic areas of the West Bank was taking place in the aftermath of the ICJ advisory opinion and General Assembly Resolution ES-10/15, in which all 25 EU countries had joined the overwhelming majority in demanding that Israel comply with the ICJ opinion. Israeli officials feared that the European Union would go further at the next meeting of the General Assembly in September 2004 and support a resolution calling for sanctions against Israel. Fears of punitive action because of Israel's refusal to comply with the advisory opinion appeared justified: in August the Non-Aligned Movement had urged all its 115 member states to impose sanctions against Israeli settlements and 'companies and entities involved in construction of the wall'. Alarmed at the prospect of further sanctions, a Ministry of Justice legal team recommended that Israel formally adopt the Fourth Geneva Convention to draw the sting out of international criticism. The Foreign Ministry was even more pessimistic, forecasting that the European Union might delay Israel's entry into the European Neighbourhood Policy, halt funding to the Palestinian Authority so that Israel would have to bear the humanitarian cost, or most damaging of all, suspend its Association Agreement with Israel.[66]

In the event, none of these fears came to pass. Sharon himself had no doubts as to the reason: 'Without that readiness [to disengage], we would be facing very heavy pressure. Israel has no pressures today.'[67] But inactivity was also attributable to a lack of will on the part of the international community, especially the Europeans, to go beyond the customary declarations and demarches. The background to the unanimous EU support for General Assembly Resolution ES-10/15 revealed less of a principled stand than first appeared: up to an hour before the vote the EU ambassadors had decided to abstain, until persuaded by Sweden, and especially France, to support the decision.[68] Once the General Assembly reconvened in September, far from pushing for follow-up action, the European Union made clear that the issue should be pursued no further at the United Nations. '"We are not interested to continue dealing with the issue of the separation fence within the parameters of the United Nations," one EU diplomat said. "The [ICJ] opinion is advisory and does not require that deliberations on the issue continue in the General Assembly."' [69]

If a symbol was needed of the international community's desire to sideline the issue of the wall as the disengagement bandwagon rolled on, it was furnished by Kofi Annan during his visit to Israel and the West Bank in February 2005. Despite the fact that the United Nations' highest judicial body, the ICJ, had ruled that the wall was in violation of international law and demanded its removal, the Secretary-General did not find it appropriate to visit the wall during his trip or to meet with Palestinians affected by it. Indeed, by June 2005 the mood at the United Nations had changed to such an extent that Israel's ambassador Dan Gillerman was elected one of the vice presidents for the next meeting of the General Assembly, the same body that had censured Israel by such an overwhelming majority less than a year before.[70] By September 2005, Sharon was the star guest at the World Summit to celebrate the sixtieth anniversary of the United Nations, at which he addressed the General Assembly, and Israel was announcing its candidacy for one of the rotating seats on the Security Council in 2019. In the face of these developments, Palestinian attempts to convene either an emergency General Assembly session or a Security Council meeting to mark the first anniversary of the ICJ advisory opinion in July 2005 were stymied by lack of support from member countries.[71]

By the time that Sharon paid an official visit to President Bush in April 2005, he had every reason to feel pleased by the strategic gains resulting from the disengagement plan. It was true that the United States had not automatically underwritten all of his aims vis-à-vis the wall: the route had been brought closer to the Green Line in certain areas, some enclaves were removed and there was a definite veto on exploiting the wall to invoke the Absentee Property Law to dispossess Palestinian farmers of their lands within the Jerusalem Envelope. The United States was also irritated at Sharon's revival of the dormant E1 Plan – his approval of the construction of 3,500 new housing units in the area between Maale Adumim and Jerusalem in March 2005. US protests were pro-forma, however, and there was no talk of penalties. Most importantly, Sharon had US commitment to support Israel's retention of the settlement blocs in the form of a written pledge from Bush, and US approval for a wall that encompassed the blocs: 'no one sitting at this table has achieved what I have', he boasted at a cabinet meeting, referring to the letter.[72]

Over the years the US position on settlements had steadily been eroded to Israel's advantage; from 'contrary to international law' under the Carter administration, to an 'obstacle to peace' under Bush Senior to 'unhelpful' by the time of the Clinton administration.[73] The Bush administration, in this as in other

Open Letter to Kofi Annan[74]

From Israeli and Palestinian and international peace activists

Dear Secretary-General Annan,

We welcome you to Israel–Palestine. Your interviews in the Israeli media suggest you are attempting to address negative attitudes towards the United Nations prevalent among many Israelis – an important goal, whose achievement may facilitate a more effective UN role as part of the international 'Quartet' charged with promoting an end to the Israeli-Palestinian conflict. Your decision to attend the ceremony at Yad Vashem Holocaust Museum in Jerusalem is evidently part of that effort, and a renewed affirmation of the United Nations's determination to oppose any manifestation of racial prejudice and persecution, of which the extermination of six million European Jews is a particularly horrific and terrible example.

Nevertheless, your visit takes place at a particularly sensitive time, when every action has most serious long-term ramifications. Precisely because of the importance of your visit here, the choice to include certain sites on your itinerary and exclude others is crucial. As you told Israeli TV recently, the Gaza Disengagement Plan propounded by PM Sharon could be a positive step – provided it is a step in the implementation of the 'Road Map,' whose ultimate goal is viable peace, a complete end to the Occupation and the creation of a viable Palestine.

Unfortunately, there is no sign that Ariel Sharon regards things that way; there are many signs to the contrary: not only explicit statements by Sharon and his aides expressing a clear intention to hold on to the bulk of the West Bank lands, but also unilateral acts on the ground intended to grab Palestinian territory and effectively annex it to Israel.

In particular, we wish to stress continuing construction of the so-called 'Separation Wall.' All across the West Bank, entire communities are being cordoned off, many losing their land. . . . Palestinian towns, especially around Jerusalem (e.g. Abu Dis, Bethlehem and A-Ram) are being cut down the middle or surrounded and made into isolated enclaves, with a massive dislocation of trade, education, health services, access to religious sites and every facet of normal daily life. . . . At Jayous village, where the Wall was erected in 2003, one can see settlers busily creating a new settlement on land to which the Palestinian owners are denied access – in the so-called 'Seam Zone.' This political border (the real intention of the Wall) is creating conditions whereby settlements thrive and expand while Palestinians are fearful of being forced into transfer: a form of ethnic cleansing.

Your visit to Jerusalem, passing within a short distance of where all this takes place, without stopping to acknowledge it, will be construed as tacit acquiescence by you and the institution you head – tacit acquiescence in a brutal practice for which the security of Israelis is the pretext rather than the true reason; security can only be reached by a political solution and the Wall actually hampers rather than helps reach such a solution.

We need hardly remind you that the creation of this Wall was strongly condemned by the overwhelming majority of the UN General Assembly, that its disastrous humanitarian consequences have been elaborated in great detail by a UN Rapporteur and that its continuing creation is in flagrant defiance of the International Court at The Hague, the body empowered by the international community to interpret International Law. We are sure it is not your intention to approve – explicitly or tacitly – such phenomena. Nevertheless, that is what you would be doing in practice by failing to include the Wall on the itinerary of your visit. Therefore, we –

Israeli and Palestinian and international peace activists – call upon you to observe first-hand the Wall and its disastrous humanitarian effects, which will have such a negative impact on peace making and the future viability of Palestine. We also eagerly await institution of a Register of Damages caused by the Wall, and the institution of a system of compensation for loss of income, education, freedom of movement, land and homes, as called for by the ICJ Advisory Opinion and UN General Assembly.

spheres, carried this disregard of international law one step further by endorsing the eventual annexation of the settlement blocs to Israel. It was true that Bush's letter stipulated that annexation should be by agreement between the two parties, but in the long interim period their *de facto* annexation could proceed apace, fortified by their new status of being located on the Israeli side of the wall.

If the United States was complicit in Sharon's designs vis-à-vis the wall and the settlement blocs, and the United Nations ineffective in the face of Security Council vetoes and member states' reluctance to implement the advisory opinion, what of the European Union? Since the time of the Venice Declaration of 1980, which endorsed the Palestinians' right to self-determination, the European Union had been instrumental in establishing what is now the international consensus for a resolution of the conflict through a two-state solution on the basis of the pre-1967 borders. Unlike the United States, the European Union paid due respect to human rights and international law, and consistently condemned settlements and the wall. It also had political and economic leverage, being Israel's most important trading partner and also the largest donor to the Palestinians, thus relieving Israel of most of its responsibilities under the Fourth Geneva Convention for ensuring the welfare of the population under occupation. The EU-Israel Association Agreement granted preferential trading status, and Israel was in the first 'basket' of countries applying for membership of the European Neighbourhood Policy, the highest level of partnership possible for a non-EU country. That Israel took these political and economic ties seriously was demonstrated by its dismay when all 25 EU members voted in favour of General Assembly Resolution ES-10/15, which demanded that Israel comply with the ICJ advisory opinion. With rumours of sanctions by the European Union, for the first time the prospect dawned on Israel that there might be a diplomatic – and perhaps political and economic – price to pay for its non-compliance with international law.

It was not even necessary for a proactive campaign of sanctions to be initiated: the treaties that the European Union had signed with Israel in themselves contained the appropriate clauses for punitive action. In particular, Article 2 of the EU-Israel Association Agreement stated that 'Relations between the Parties, as well as the provisions of the Agreement itself, shall be based [on] respect for human rights and democratic principles'. The ICJ found that the wall violated both international humanitarian law and the major international human rights treaties, and called on all states 'not to recognise the illegal situation resulting from the construction of the wall'. Given that Israel was in violation of 'an essential element' of its own signed commitments under the Association Agreement, was the European Union not bound both by its own contractual undertakings and its declared adherence to international law to invoke punitive measures, such as suspension or part suspension of the Agreement, as had been proposed by the UN Special Rapporteur on the Right to Food?

Instead of confronting Israel, the European Union resorted to its old policy of trying to exert pressure through quiet diplomacy. During a debate on the wall in the European Parliament, a Green Party MEP demanded in exasperation: 'Those people who say that instead we should be relying on European pressure on Israel should tell me when European pressure alone on Israel has ever yielded any results – it has not.'[75] For all that, the carrot rather than the stick was employed, with Israel becoming more integrated into EU networks during 2004, and concluding a new agreement on scientific and technological cooperation in April that year.

Disengagement became another excuse to avoid confronting Israel over its continuing wall construction and settlement expansion, actions that were in clear violation of the European Union's own stated objectives for resolving the conflict. Even as it became evident that withdrawal from Gaza was a manoeuvre to consolidate Israel's hold over the 'inseparable parts' of the West Bank and East Jerusalem, there was no substantive reaction from the European Union. Settlement construction and wall expansion evoked only the standard protests, including the futile assertion that 'no party should take unilateral steps that could prejudge the results of the final negotiations'.[76] The European Union appeared content to leave international political leverage on Israel to the United States, resorting to its normal, passive 'payer not player' role, even as the paying increased due to the increased humanitarian costs of the wall.[77]

A year after the ICJ advisory opinion, Justice Minister Lapid need not have worried about Israel becoming the 'new South Africa' and facing an international campaign of boycotts and sanctions. The only demand for such measures was coming from the Non-Aligned Movement and from church groups and non-state actors. Far from becoming an international outlaw Israel enjoyed greater participation in international bodies such as the United Nations than at any time since the beginning of the second *intifada*. If the international community had largely failed the Palestinians with regard to the wall and the implementation of the ICJ advisory opinion, what scope was there for non-state actors?

NOTES

1.   Robin Cook, 'Bush will now celebrate by putting Falluja to the torch', *The Guardian*, 5 November 2004.

2.   Aluf Benn, 'Analysis: up against the fence', *Ha'aretz*, 30 June 2003.

3.   Ibid.

4.   White House Press Release, 'President Bush welcomes Prime Minister Abbas to White House'. <http://www.whitehouse.gov/news/releases/2003/07/20030725-6.html> (accessed on 18 October 2005).

5.   White House Press Release, 'President discusses Middle East peace with Prime Minister Sharon'. <http://www.whitehouse.gov/news/releases/2003/07/20030729-2.html> (accessed on 18 October 2005).

6.   UN Secretary-General, 'Secretary-General disturbed by Israel's decisions on separation wall, new settlements', SG/SM/8913, 2 October 2003. 'EU: Israel must stop building fence beyond Green Line border', Reuters, 9 October 2004.

7.   By his own recollection, 'Dubi' (Weisglass) had monthly meetings with 'Condy' during his tenure as Sharon's bureau chief and was often in daily telephone contact. Ari Shavit, 'The big freeze', *Ha'aretz*, 8 October 2004.

8.   'Powell: US has no plans to penalize Israel for fence route', Reuters, 9 April 2004.

9.   '"When there was a sense that the road map was a viable option, and that Mahmoud Abbas's [Abu Mazen's] reformed government seemed to be in full bloom this summer, there was a sense in Washington that the mere existence of the fence was objectionable because it could hurt him," said David Makovsky, a scholar at the Washington Institute for Near East Policy. "However, as these prospects faded, the debate (in Washington) very much has evolved . . . to a more nuanced debate over the direction of the fence."' Ori Nir, 'Bush drops opposition to building of barrier: fence gains nod as road map dies', *Forward*, 24 October 2003.

10. Marc Carnegie, 'US vetoes resolution condemning Israeli security wall', Agence France-Presse, 14 October 2003.

11. UN General Assembly resolution E-10/13 of 21 October 2003.

12. Statement by Minister Roche at the European Parliament, on behalf of the Council of Ministers, on the EU position on the hearing of the International Court of Justice on the Israeli Wall, 11 February 2004.

13. Report of the Secretary-General pursuant to General Assembly resolution ES-10/13 of 24 November 2003, para 29.

14. ACRI Press Release, 'Separation barrier route violates international law', 5 May 2005.

15. B'Tselem, Land Grab, p. 48.

16. Article 55 (b) of the Regulations Attached to the Hague Convention (IV) Respecting the Laws and Customs of War on Land; Fourth Geneva Convention Relative to the Protection of Civilian Persons in Time of War, Article 49 (6).

17. B'Tselem, Land Grab, p. 51.

18. Mazal Mualem, 'Inner cabinet to discuss Lapid's changes to fence', Ha'aretz, 16 January 2004.

19. Aluf Benn and Gideon Alon, 'Gov't to examine changes in West Bank separation fence', Ha'aretz, 19 January 2004.

20. Itamar Eichner, 'The Fence', Yedioth Ahronoth, 15 January 2004.

21. Ilil Shahar, 'Israel plans to paint separation fence', Ma'ariv, 9 February 2004.

22. Yuval Yoaz, 'State tells High Court fence route is being 'reassessed'', Ha'aretz, 10 February 2004.

23. Amnon Barzilai and Amir Oren, 'Defense officials ask for money to "minimize fence's harm to Palestinians"', Ha'aretz, 9 February 2004.

24. Amnon Barzilai, 'PM adviser: no plans for "eastern fence" in West Bank', Ha'aretz, 10 March 2004.

25. Ilil Shahar, 'Poll: near majority of Americans support the separation fence', Ma'ariv, 27 January 2004.

26. Ian Williams, 'Israeli wall on trial: venue shifts to the International Court of Justice', Foreign Policy In Focus Commentary, 10 February 2004. 'However, [Dershowitz's] attachment to international and domestic law is such that he has favorably considered torture for suspected terrorists, and random destruction of Palestinian villages in retaliation for suicide bombing attacks, so Israel has quite wisely not made him its advocate before the Tribunal.'

27. Janine Zacharia 'Kerry defends security fence', *Jerusalem Post*, 25 February 2004.

28. Aluf Benn, 'Israel wants US report held until after Hague hearing', *Ha'aretz*, 2 February 2004. According to one authority, in the past the 'State Department has even allowed Israeli officials to review and edit its human rights report on Israeli practices in the occupied territories prior to its publication, substantially toning down the original analysis'. Stephen Zunes, *Tinderbox: US Middle East Policy and the Roots of Terrorism*, (Zed Books, 2003), p. 12.

29. However, the US contention, in its written submission, that 'it would be inconsistent with the resolutions of the Security Council and the General Assembly, and create a serious risk to the peace process, if any party unilaterally or this court, were to seek to undermine the outcome of any of the permanent status issues' was astonishing, both in its concern for the UN resolutions which Israel had violated over the years with US connivance, and the claim that the advisory opinion, and not the wall, would prejudice progress towards a negotiated settlement. US submission, para. 1.6. <http://www.icj-cij.org/icjwww/idocket/imwp/imwpframe.htm> (Written Statements, then United States of America) (accessed on 21 October 2005).

30. Quoted in Euro-Mediterranean Human Rights Network, 'A human rights review on the EU and Israel: relating commitments to actions, 2003–2004', December 2004, p. 54. <http://www.euromedrights.net/english/emhrn-documents/File/HR%20Review%20on%20EU%20and%20Israel_final_ENG.doc> (accessed on 24 October 2005).

31. Tali Nir, 'World Court hearings on separation fence enter third and last day', *Ha'aretz*, 25 February 2004.

32. Nina Gilbert, 'Israel readies for PR blitz in The Hague', *Jerusalem Post*, 17 February 2004.

33. Yoel Marcus, 'Down and out in The Hague', *Ha'aretz*, 27 February 2004.

34. The principal reports were: Amnesty International, *Israel and the Occupied Territories: The Place of the Fence/Wall in International Law*, 19 February 2004; Human Right Watch, *Israel's 'Separation Barrier' in the Occupied West Bank: Human Rights and International Human Law Consequences*, February 2004; Oxford Public Interest Lawyers (OXPIL), *Legal Consequences of Israel's Construction of a Separation Barrier in the Occupied Territories: International Law Opinion*, University of Oxford, February 2000 (<http://student.cs.ucc.ie/cs1064/jabowen/IPSC/articles/oxpilSummary.pdf#search='OXPIL'>,

accessed on 21 October 2005); International Commission of Jurists, Geneva, *Israel's Separation Barrier: Challenges to the rule of law and human rights*, (undated); and Harvard University's *Program on Humanitarian Policy and Conflict Research, The Separation Barrier and International Humanitarian Law*, <http://www.ihlresearch.org/opt/>.

35. Press release No. 04/12, 18 February 2004.
36. Para. 65.
37. Para. 137.
38. Paras. 111-113.
39. Paras 78, 101.
40. Para. 120.
41. Paras.122, 134.
42. Para. 121.
43. Paras. 137, 142.
44. Para. 163.
45. Paras 152, 153.
46. Para. 159.
47. 'After court rules fence is illegal, battleground shifts to UN', *Ha'aretz*, 10 July 2004.
48. Janine Zacharia, 'US slams "misuse" of ICJ', *Jerusalem Post*, 15 July 2004.
49. The EU Council of Ministers, through the Irish presidency, stipulated 'five elements' to make the unilateral disengagement acceptable to the international community: it must take place in the context of the Road Map; it must be a step towards a two-state solution; it must not involve a transfer of settlement activity to the West Bank; there must be an organised and negotiated handover of responsibility to the Palestinian Authority; and Israel must facilitate the rehabilitation and reconstruction of Gaza. Brian Cowen, 'Road map to Middle East peace needs a new start', *Irish Times*, 27 February 2004.
50. Shavit, 'The big freeze.'
51. Ibid.
52. 'State: W. Bank settler population grew by 12,800 last year.' *Ha'aretz*, 27 August 2005.
53. Ibid. Weisglass is referring to the number of settlers in the West Bank, excluding Jerusalem, whom Israel has no intention of ever removing.
54. Ibid.
55. Text of letter from President Bush to Prime Minister Sharon, 15 April 2004.

56. Steven Erlanger, 'Israel adds to plans for more housing units in settlements', *New York Times*, 24 August 2004.

57. Aluf Benn and Yuval Yoaz, 'Israel asks for US endorsement of fence route', *Ha'aretz*, 31 March 2004.

58. Akiva Eldar, 'US experts doubt need for airport fence', *Ha'aretz*, 5 November 2004.

59. Arieh O'Sullivan, 'PM "drags feet" on southern fence', *Jerusalem Post*, 10 December 2003.

60. Aluf Benn, Amos Harel and Arnon Regular, 'PM to use pullout to neutralize criticism of fence', *Ha'aretz*, 15 February 2005.

61. Herb Keinon, 'UK protests Ma'aleh Adumim fence route', *Jerusalem Post*, 1 March 2005.

62. Aluf Benn, 'Drawing the line', *Ha'aretz*, 25 March 2005.

63. Herb Keinon, 'PM: West Bank settlements to expand', *Jerusalem Post*, 22 August 2005.

64. Meron Rappaport and Yuval Yoaz, 'With pullout past, IDF moves to fence Ma'aleh Adumim', *Ha'aretz*, 24 August 2005.

65. Aluf Benn, 'Sharon ordered E-1 police HQ built two months ago', *Ha'aretz*, 26 August 2005.

66. Aluf Benn, 'Foreign Ministry fears EU sanctions over policy in territories', Ha'aretz, 17 October 2004.

67. David Horovitz and Herb Keinon, 'Sharon speaks to the "*Post*"', *Jerusalem Post*, 22 April 2005.

68. Shlomo Shamir, 'FM: EU vote encourages PA to avoid fighting terror', *Ha'aretz*, 22 July 2004.

69. Shlomo Shamir, 'EU opposed to more talks on fence at UN', *Ha'aretz*, 15 September 2004.

70. Israel's candidacy was supported by the 'Western European and Others' regional grouping within the General Assembly, which in addition to the countries of Western Europe includes the United States, Canada, Australia and New Zealand. Shlomo Shamir, 'Israeli envoy to be next vice president of UN General Assembly', *Ha'aretz*, 14 June 2005.

71. Shlomo Shamir, 'PA seeks UN condemnation of fence', *Ha'aretz*, 18 July 2005.

72. Aluf Benn, 'Ranch burgers', *Ha'aretz*, 1 April 2005.

73. Zunes, *Tinderbox*, p. 129.

74. The open letter was signed by Palestinian, Israeli and international activists. Various authors, 'Open Letter to Kofi Annan', <http://electronic intifada.net/v2/article3691.shtml> (accessed on 18 October 2005). During

[184]

his visit to meet with Abu Mazen in Ramallah, the Secretary-General was met by Palestinians protesting against his refusal to visit the wall.

75. Green Party MEP Caroline Lucas, quoted in Euro-Mediterranean Human Rights Network, 'A human rights review on the EU and Israel', p. 54.

76. EU press release, 'Presidency "deeply concerned" by Maale Adumim building plans', 5 April 2004.

77. '"We believe this wall creates many additional humanitarian problems and additional costs to our own operations," said Cees Wittebrood, head of European Humanitarian Aid Office (ECHO) operations in the Middle East and Mediterranean. "We calculated that some 20 per cent is needed additionally to face the humanitarian consequences of this fence," Wittebrood told a news conference late on Saturday.' Reuters, 'EU says Israel's security fence adds to aid costs', 26 Jan 2004.

A farmer waiting for the gate to open near Yabad, West Bank

5 Activism and Advocacy

'JUSTICE, GAS AND TEARS'

In a story that offers few glimmers of justice or optimism, the account in the box below of a demonstration in A-Ram, Jerusalem, by a participant from the Israeli peace group, Gush Shalom, strikes a singularly positive note. Joint, non-violent protest against the wall proved that there were some Palestinians and Israelis who could 'still live together', three years into a conflict that had led to thousands of fatalities and caused bitterness and distrust on both sides. With the sharp rightward shift of Israeli society during the second *intifada*, the few Israeli peace and rights groups still engaged had become – by default – 'far left', with a corresponding increase in their activism and humanitarian interventions.[1] The activists and groups protesting against the wall ventured not just to the relatively safe environs of Jerusalem but to the most remote West Bank villages, officially off-limits to Israeli citizens because of security concerns. Their reception by Palestinians was 'completely positive – almost overwhelmingly so' in the words of a member of the so-called 'Anarchists Against The Wall', the most radical of the new groups.[2]

Away from the frontline, there were also a number of instances where residents of Israeli communities joined in common cause against the wall with their Palestinian neighbours across the Green Line. In the landmark Beit Sourik case,

Demonstration in A-Ram (1)[3]

Once again, the organisers underestimated the number of people who would come to participate in a protest against the monstrous wall which the Sharon government seems bent on erecting. The pundits who make self-satisfied statements about Israelis and Palestinians being 'too alienated from each other to ever live together' and draw the conclusion that 'a civilised divorce is the best which could be hoped for' should have seen the merging of these two groups. At one moment there were two distinct groups – some 2,000 Palestinians forging ahead, 500 Israelis quickly catching up with them. The next, the two flowed smoothly into each other and became a single mass, above which flew in profusion, and in no particular order, Hebrew and Arabic and English signs and flags and the emblems of Israeli peace groups and Arab parties from Israel and the main factions of the Palestinian political spectrum all side by side, Gush Shalom and Fatah and Hadash and Yesh Gvul and the Israeli Women's Coalition and Palestinian Islamists (only a few of them, but quite distinct) and Knesset Member Azmi Bishara's Balad Party . . . and a sizeable block of the red flags of the Palestinian People's Party (former Communists), and among them a solitary flag of the Italian communists, flown by a visiting delegation. And the Ecumenical Accompaniers of the World [Council of] Churches have all gathered here from the various towns and villages where they fulfil various tasks, and people from the International Solidarity Movement and the Christian Peacemakers, and some of the Japanese who recently seem to crop up at virtually every peace demonstration.

There was a considerable presence of Palestinian women, young and old, some dressed in demure traditional clothes while others were clad in the latest of western fashions.. . .A group of girls were marching under a hand-drawn banner, 'Break the Wall'.. . . They were, it turned out, from 'The Bridge

Academy', an institute which stands to suffer a mortal blow from the Wall. 'Half of us are from A-Ram here, the others from Beit Hanina across the highway. Until now we went back and forth without even thinking about it, but if they build the wall across the highway we will not be able to meet each other again, and our school will lose half of its pupils . . .'

Israelis from the Israeli town of Mevasseret Zion (in addition to high-ranking ex-military and intelligence personnel from the left-leaning Council for Peace and Security) joined in the Beit Sourik's Village Council petition to the High Court. Apart from the practical achievements – the Israeli High Court ordered major changes to the proposed route in the Beit Sourik area because of the disproportionate harm the wall would cause to local Palestinians – such gestures were important for morale. 'With all their distress and worry, the unexpected support from Mevasseret Zion has produced a spark of hope among the villagers [of Beit Sourik]. They feel less alone on the battle-field.'[4] The phenomenon, however, should not be overesti-mated: the vast majority of Israelis continued to support construction of the wall, regardless of its location and its impact on Palestinians. Nevertheless, mobilisation against the wall became the most sustained example of Israeli-Palestinian cooperation to come out of the second *intifada*.

The emergence of a corps of Israeli anti-wall activists – as distinct from Israelis who had previously joined in the protests of the International Solidarity Movement – dates from the joint Palestinian-Israeli 'peace camp' set up in the West Bank village of Masha, which attracted over 1,000 Israeli participants throughout late 2003.[5] Circumstances were now more favourable than had been the case a year earlier for the unfortunate farmers in the northern West Bank. Their non-violent protests had been ineffective in halting or significantly influencing the route of the wall, despite support from international activists from the International Solidarity Movement, the International Women's Peace Service and the Ecumenical Accompaniers of the World Council of Churches. By late 2003, there was much more international focus on the wall in the wake of the imminent ICJ proceedings. In addition, the belated intervention of the Israeli High Court in the Beit Sourik case offered some hope of redress for Palestinian concerns. Greater media and legal scrutiny, High Court petitions and interim injunctions, and joint Palestinian, Israeli and international protests could now combine to some effect, at least at the local level. In villages close to the Green Line there was perhaps greater potential for cross-community cooperation, in that many older Palestinians had worked in Israel before the second *intifada* and drew a distinction between ordinary Israelis and IDF soldiers.[6] In the main, these villages had also been spared the military offensives inflicted by the IDF on the major West Bank and Gaza Strip cities and refugee camps.

The village of Budrus in the Ramallah district proved the inspiration for what was termed a 'third uprising' and was, in the words of one of the main organisers of the local protests, 'an *intifada* with an approach based entirely on peaceful confrontation'.[7] If the route went ahead as planned, Budrus would lose most of what little land had not already been ceded to Israel in 1948. Together with eight neighbouring villages, Budrus would also be enclosed within a double barrier. Accordingly, 'popular committees' were formed in the nine villages, uniting all the political factions as well as women's and youth groups. All sectors of society were encouraged to participate in the demonstrations, including women, who organised their own protest marches with the participation of Israeli and foreign women.

The emphasis was on peaceful action with all manifestations of violence, including stone throwing, discouraged. It was also emphasised that the protests were against a wall that threatened the agricultural lands on which the village depended: it was not against Israel and the participation of Israeli supporters was encouraged.

The protests remained largely peaceful despite the IDF's swift resort to rubber bullets and teargas, the punitive incursions at night into the village to arrest activists, and the imposition of curfews, closed military zones and deportation orders to deter the Israeli and foreign activists. The Israeli security forces also attempted to decapitate the movement by arresting the main organisers, Ayed Morrar and his brother, on manifestly false charges.[8] Months of protests against the bulldozers paid off: the wall was re-routed, thus saving the bulk of Budrus's agricultural land. The plan for double barriers was also dropped, perhaps as much due to US rejection of the Israeli claim that a second barrier was necessary to protect Ben-Gurion airport as to the influence of the local protests. A sign of the growing interest in non-violent activism was the attendance of thousands of Palestinians at rallies by Arun Gandhi, grandson of Mahatma Gandhi and world-renowned advocate of non-violence, during his visit to the West Bank in summer 2004. Weariness with the armed struggle also played a part and by 2005 there were even indications that Hamas, not known for its fondness for non-violent action or its willingness to cooperate with Israelis, was prepared to consider non-violent struggle, if not as the sole means, at least as an alternative to military action.[9]

The dilemma for Palestinian advocates of non-violence was that, in most cases, peaceful protest met with no equivalent response on the part of the Israeli security forces. The presence of internationals in anti-wall demonstrations, in addition to

Demonstration in A-Ram (2)[10]

In the centre of A-Ram, thousands of Palestinians were waiting for us. The demonstration was intended, of course, to be completely non-violent. The proof: in the first line there marched a Christian Orthodox priest, a senior Muslim sheikh, local dignitaries and present and past members of the Knesset and the Palestinian parliament. In front of us walked the A-Ram youth orchestra. As a symbolic act we had brought five big hammers, and some of the demonstrators were asked to use them to strike concrete slabs lying on the ground.

We advanced slowly in the burning sun. Suddenly a row of border-policemen appeared on top of the hill overlooking the road. Before we realised what was happening, a salvo of teargas grenades – one, two, three . . . dozens – were shot at us. In a few moments we were enveloped by a dense cloud of gas that covered all escape routes. We dispersed in all directions, but the gas grenades continued to explode around us. Those of us who made it to the central square of the town were attacked with tear gas, water cannon and rubber-coated bullets. The place resembled a real battlefield – clouds of gas, the sound of exploding stun grenades and shooting, the screaming sirens of the Palestinian ambulances, burning boxes along the street, abandoned posters, shuttered shops. When the Palestinian paramedics started to run with their stretchers towards the ambulances, local boys emerged from the alleys to throw stones at the border-policemen (a mercenary force universally hated in the Palestinian territories). From time to time groups of border-policemen ran towards us, grabbing demonstrators of both sexes and dragging them towards the armoured jeeps. One of the ambulances was burning. Undercover policemen in plain clothes, pistols in their hands, beat people and dragged them along the ground. All this continued for more than two hours. All that time a question was nagging me: Why was this happening? Clearly we had walked into a well-prepared trap. But what was the aim?

On the way back we listened to the news on the radio. A police spokesman announced that the border-police had been attacked by demonstrators who threw axes and hammers at them. In our bus, everybody burst out laughing. The mystery was solved two days later in court, when the judges were dealing with A-Ram. The government attorneys demanded that the temporary injunction that was holding up the wall in A-Ram be lifted. They had a crushing argument: two days ago, they said, the border-policemen guarding the machinery had been viciously attacked by demonstrators. Their lives were in danger. Therefore, in order to save the policemen from the evildoers (us), the building of the wall must be speeded up.

expressing solidarity and increasing international attention, was intended to furnish a measure of protection to the Palestinians concerned: 'When they [the IDF] see a foreign activist in front of the bulldozers, they take care,' one demonstrator explained. 'If they were not here, it would be more violent. Maybe they would kill me.'[11] In theory, the presence of Israeli participants among the demonstrators should have provided an extra layer of immunity, in that IDF soldiers would be even more reluctant to employ force against their compatriots, however much they might disapprove of their views and activities. As it turned out, the assumption that the presence of international protestors would automatically have a deterrent effect on the IDF was mistaken. Nor did the appearance of Israeli activists in the frontline always prevent violence against Palestinians or the Israelis themselves.

The reality was that the Israeli security forces responded with overwhelming and disproportionate force not only to Palestinian violence, but also when Palestinians employed non-violent means of protest.

Typical of such reactions was what happened at the second Ram demonstration as described by veteran peace campaigner, Uri Avnery in the box on page 192. If such a response by the Border Police could occur in Jerusalem, in the presence of the media and where Israeli law applied, it was not difficult to imagine the situation in remote West Bank villages, where protestors were confronted by the Border Police and IDF operating in a culture of almost total impunity.[12] Although no arms were employed by Palestinian protestors against the Israeli security forces in over three years of anti-wall protests, nine Palestinians were shot dead and hundreds were injured. It is true that Palestinian protests often ended in stone throwing by youths, which could result in injury to IDF soldiers, but such incidents usually occurred after the IDF had already resorted to force.[13] There were also documented cases where undercover Israeli security forces disguised as demonstrators provoked clashes by throwing stones at soldiers.[14] Indeed, an investigation by the Israeli newspaper *Ha'aretz* into the violent suppression of demonstrations in the West Bank village of Bil'in, which succeeded Budrus as the main centre for anti-wall protests, found that the Border Police 'have made false accusations against demonstrators and even made arrests on the basis of those accusations'.[15]

Nor did foreign activists always escape without injury. Rachel Corrie and Tom Hundall were killed by the IDF in Gaza in incidents not related to the wall, and other members of the International Solidarity Movement were injured in anti-wall protests, in addition to the more than 60 deported and 100 denied entry to the country. Although there was generally more tolerant behaviour towards Israeli protestors, this was not always the case, as demonstrated by the injury by live rounds of one of the 'anarchists', Gil Na'amati in December 2003. Although the IDF banned the firing of live ammunition at Israeli demonstrators following the Na'amati shooting, Israeli protestors continue to be subject to mistreatment by Israeli security forces.[16] Some suspected something more ominous than the usual over-reaction of occupation soldiers: 'From Sharon's vantage point, nothing could be more menacing than the emergence of a nonviolent movement of civil disobedience, particularly one in which Jews and Arabs work together.'[17]

While local, international and Israeli activists were risking deportation, death and injury, the Palestinian Authority was conspicuous by its inactivity in campaigning against the wall. From the beginning it was local activists, with the support of foreign sympathisers in the International Solidarity Movement, who brought news of the impact of the wall at the local level to the attention of a wider audience. Even when it became evident that the wall posed serious problems at a national level, it was left to civil society actors such as the Palestinian Environmental NGO Network, PENGON, to mobilise nationwide. The PENGON anti-apartheid wall campaign also undertook international outreach and advocacy initiatives, such as inaugurating 9 November, the anniversary of the fall of the Berlin Wall, as the starting day for the international week against the wall.[18] By early 2003, foreign journalists, the locally based international organisations monitoring the humanitarian situation – UNRWA, the World Bank and UNOCHA – and the Israeli human rights group B'Tselem, in addition to PENGON, had produced articles, reports, impact studies and maps, but there was still almost total silence on the part of the Palestinian Authority.[19]

It was almost a year into construction, in mid-2003, before the Palestinian Authority reacted with any sense of urgency and Abu Mazen, in his capacity as the first Palestinian prime minister, raised the issue of the wall in his meetings with President Bush and Condoleeza Rice. Even this was only after the anti-wall campaign had organised a sit-in of angry farmers in his Ramallah office. Anger on the part of rural communities at their apparent abandonment by the Palestinian Authority remains strong, compounded by the revelation that Palestinian cement companies, including one owned by Abu Mazen's successor as prime minister, Ahmed Qureia, have allegedly been implicated in supplying cement for settlements and for the wall.[20] Official inaction may be due to Palestinian Authority officials having 'no affinity or relation with the people' in the words of one critic.[21] Others see more sinister motives, alleging that the Palestinian Authority is prepared to sacrifice the 10 per cent of West Bank territory cut off by the wall in the belief that the remainder can be salvaged for the future Palestinian state. Whatever the reason, in the absence of a central authority to organise, finance and guide a national campaign against the wall, successes have been limited to the local level, for all the efforts of committed local activists and their supporters. Nor is there any indication, despite the moral and legal victory that the ICJ advisory opinion and General Assembly Resolution ES-10/15 represent, that the Palestinian Authority is prepared to declare Israel's continuing construction of the wall and related settlement activity a 'red line', in the face of which peace negotiations are impossible.

CONCLUSION: 'FAILING THE MORAL TEST'

The ICJ advisory opinion, and General Assembly Resolution ES-10/15, not only condemned the route of the wall as illegal but clearly set out the obligations incumbent on UN member states to ensure compliance by Israel. However, apart from a call for sanctions by the Non-Aligned Movement at the state level, it has been non-state actors that have called for penalties such as selective divestment from Israel in response to its refusal to comply with the ICJ ruling, and related violations of international law. In particular, it has been progressive faith-based organisations, such as the World Council of Churches, that have urged members to sell off investments in companies profiting from Israel's actions in the West Bank and Gaza Strip.[22] Otherwise, given the failure of the international community to live up to its commitments, it has been individuals who have cited the moral authority of the ICJ advisory opinion, as Pat O'Connor of the International Solidarity Movement did, for example, in his (unsuccessful) appeal against deportation on the charge of organising and participating in 'illegal demonstrations' against the wall.

At the official level, the only practical step resulting from either the ICJ advisory opinion or Resolution ES-10/15 was the decision in January 2005 by the UN Secretary-General to set up a 'Register of Damage' to compensate Palestinians affected by the wall. The functions of the register are vague. It is not clear how 'damage' will be defined and 'the register's purpose is merely to collect claims for possible future adjudication and compensation'.[23] In any case, the process of establishing the register 'appears to have been lost in the bureaucracy of the United Nations'.[24] Given Israel's continuing failure as occupying power to meet its responsibility to ensure the welfare of the Palestinian

Israel is failing the moral test[25]

Pat O'Connor

According to Israeli authorities, one reason for my arrest two weeks ago in Biddu and my denial of entry into Israel in 2003 is that I 'organized and participated in illegal demonstrations.' Israeli authorities frequently use the term 'illegal demonstrations' to describe peaceful protests against Israeli government violations of international law. This twisted reasoning needs to be exposed and rejected. What is legal often does not completely correspond to what is moral. However, when what is moral is described as illegal, there is a major problem. Why is it 'illegal' for hundreds of Palestinian men, women and children to march peacefully to assert their right to their land in the face of Israeli soldiers, who are defending the construction of a wall that has been declared illegal by the world's highest legal body, the International Court of Justice? Why is it 'illegal' for communities to try and implement the ICJ decision by walking together to their farmland to try peacefully to block Israeli contractors from bulldozing their land, from building a wall to cut them off from their land and from imprisoning them in their villages?

Apparently, it is forbidden for Palestinians to use the tactics of Gandhi and Martin Luther King, Jr. to try to save their land and their communities from destruction. Apparently, Israeli authorities believe that it is legal for Israeli soldiers to club Palestinian men, women and children, to use tear gas on them, shoot rubber bullets and live ammunition at them and arrest them for peacefully protesting. This use of violence against peaceful protesters is 'legal' even though the ICJ declared the construction of the wall on Palestinian land illegal. The Israeli government explains the soldiers' violence as 'Palestinian clashes with security forces,' even though the

Israeli military invariably initiates the violence and young Palestinian men only occasionally respond with rocks. According to this perspective, Israelis and internationals like me who support Palestinians in peaceful protest for legitimate rights, are acting illegally. For this reason I have been held at Ma'asiyahu Prison for more than two weeks and am awaiting deportation. I was arrested leaving the village of Biddu after planting olive tree seedlings with Palestinians, Israelis and internationals along the path that is being bulldozed for the construction of the wall through Biddu's olive groves. Nonetheless, I am proud to have nonviolently protested against the wall in Jayous, Tulkarm, Al-Zawiya, Budrus and Biddu.

In reality, nonviolent protest has been declared illegal because it is threatening for Palestinian civilians to face Israeli soldiers with a stark and public moral choice – to allow protest for legitimate rights or to crush it with military force. Unfortunately, the Israeli military and government have repeatedly failed that moral test.

population, the international community already has to bear the extra financial burden of providing humanitarian assistance to Palestinian communities affected by the wall.

In this regard, donors and implementing agencies must comply with the clause in the ICJ advisory opinion, which calls on states 'not to render aid or assistance in maintaining the situation created by such construction [of the wall]'.[26] Hence, the international community's rejection of Israel's request for funding to build tunnels, underpasses and roads as an alternative to transport networks disrupted by the wall and by settler-only roads. Although improving humanitarian conditions in the short term, an alternative transport system for Palestinians 'would perpetuate the settlements and consolidate an apartheid regime' in the words of the Palestinian Authority Planning Minister.[27] Consequently, both the Palestinian Authority and the donor and humanitarian community have drawn up guidelines to determine what type of support for wall-affected communities is consistent with the advisory opinion.[28]

For all such laudable efforts by certain parties to heed the advisory opinion, Israeli compliance is unlikely without the commitment of state and multinational actors. Despite the ICJ opinion and Resolution ES-10/15, the wall has not been stopped, nor has the completed section in the northern West Bank been dismantled. Instead, following negotiations with the US – and with the tacit agreement of the international community – the wall follows the revised route approved by the Israeli cabinet in February 2005. On the positive side, this route has resulted in the amount of land annexed *de facto* by Israel declining from the 16 per cent taken by the first route of October 2003 to approximately 10 per cent. This reduction was due, in large part, to the strong international criticism surrounding the ICJ proceedings, which also put an end to earlier initiatives to wall off the Jordan Valley. On the other hand, Israel has exploited the international goodwill resulting from the disengagement plan to include Maale Adumim settlement and large tracts of surrounding land within the revised 2005 route, territory that had not been included in the 2003 official route. Despite the implications of the Maale Adumim inclusion for the territorial integrity of a future Palestinian state and for East Jerusalem as its capital, this sleight of hand passed with virtual political and diplomatic impunity.

The revised 2005 route has resulted in the number of Palestinians trapped in closed areas dropping significantly, from 189,000 to approximately 49,000. Again this is largely because the publicity surrounding the ICJ hearings made such 'ghettoisation' difficult to defend internationally. Longer-validity permits for 'permanent residents' and extended gate opening times have eased conditions for Palestinians in the closed areas (although the advisory opinion explicitly called for the abolition of all such 'legislative and regulatory acts').[29] Despite such measures, the wall continues to have a detrimental impact on the residents of the closed areas and on the much larger number of farmers who face ever more restricted access to land and water resources isolated beyond the wall. Consequently, what the ICJ termed 'further alterations to the demographic composition of the occupied Palestinian territory', or 'voluntary' population transfer, remains a threat both for those residing in the closed areas and for those whose lands lie isolated inside.

Given these ominous trends, continuing monitoring of the impact of the wall on affected Palestinian communities remains a priority. For all the importance of humanitarian issues, however, it is essential not to lose sight of the wider context. For former US Special Middle East Envoy John Wolf, the wall came 'not under his Settlement file, but under one called Quality of Life'.[30] Both Israel and the US seek to portray any negative consequences resulting from the wall as 'humanitarian' issues, for which minor route adjustments and increased donor assistance provide the solution. However, measures such as tunnels and underpasses, while restoring some 'quality of life' to fragmented Palestinian communities, will not reconnect farmers to lands alienated by the wall. It is this land, rather than economic recovery or restored service provision, on which these communities depend for both their present livelihood and their future survival. No amount of donor aid (and it is the international community, as usual, that is bearing the humanitarian cost) will compensate for land loss. Mobile clinics are already being provided to meet the health needs of communities in the closed areas, but mobile farms are not an option for those cut off from their land.

As the settler population expands and thickens in the wall-enclosed areas and the Palestinian population declines, the wall will have long-term territorial and demographic consequences, not just at the local and regional, but at the national level. The advisory opinion warned that the wall 'along with measures taken previously . . . severely impedes the exercise by the Palestinian people of its right to self-determination'.[31] Indeed, so fundamental is the right to self-determination that the ICJ deemed Israel's violation of its obligation in this respect *erga omnes*, which '[i]n view of the importance of the rights involved, all States can be held to have a legal interest in their protection'.[32] The international community, including the United States, now accepts that 'an independent, viable, democratic and sovereign State of Palestine living side by side with Israel in peace and security' is essential for a just solution to the conflict.[33] It is unclear how such a state can emerge in a truncated West Bank, or how the Palestinian Authority can accept the virtual amputation of East Jerusalem – the state's designated capital – from the remainder of the Palestinian body politic.

In the face of these new, unilaterally imposed political realities, Palestinians will invariably be urged to seek a compromise through political negotiations. This follows a pattern: '[t]he whole thrust of Israeli and US diplomacy since Oslo has been to downplay Palestinian legal rights and to insist that negotiations between the two sides should resolve all contentious issues.'[34] Such negotiations are invariably to the further detriment of Palestinian rights, given the gross imbalance of power between the two parties and unwavering US support for Israel. According to UN Special Rapporteur

John Dugard, the Road Map follows the same trend: 'the Quartet and the road map process to which it is committed are not premised on the rule of law or respect for human rights . . . [and] the road map runs the risk of repeating the failures of the Oslo process which likewise took no account of human rights considerations.'[35]

The ICJ advisory opinion offers a corrective to this trend by re-emphasising the centrality of Palestinian legal rights. The Court rejected the contention of Israel – supported by the United States and the European Union – that the issue of the wall was of a political rather than a legal nature and therefore could be resolved through negotiations between the two parties. Noting the fundamental issues of international law at stake, the ICJ declared that 'the wall is located in a much broader frame of reference than a bilateral dispute' and is 'of particularly acute concern to the United Nations'.[36] For Professor Vaughan Lowe, chief advocate for the Palestinian case at the ICJ proceedings, the most important consequence of the advisory opinion was that it:

> established that the rights and duties of Palestine, and of Palestinians, are regulated by law and are not simply a matter for political negotiation. Palestine and Palestinians do not simply have claims and interests over which they must negotiate with Israel. They have legal rights. They do not have to bargain for these rights. They do not have to make concessions in return for recognition of those rights. They have those rights now and they are entitled to have those rights observed.[37]

Israel counters that Palestinian legal rights have been adequately addressed by the rulings of its own High Court in the Beit Sourik and Alfei Menashe cases. In both instances the Israeli High Court accepted the petitioners' arguments of disproportionate harm to the Palestinian fabric of life resulting from the wall, and ordered changes to the projected and completed routes in the locales concerned. For all the undoubted humanitarian benefits arising from these decisions, the High Court rulings contravene or ignore key ICJ pronouncements on wider legal principles, in particular that the Fourth Geneva Convention applies *de jure* to the occupied territories, including East Jerusalem, and that international human rights law is also applicable. The High Court also continues to validate construction of the wall on Palestinian territory and to deny the political intention behind the wall, despite the obvious connection between the route and settlement blocs. It should also be borne in mind that in the past the High Court 'provided the settlement enterprise with a legal stamp of approval by approving improper acts by the government and the IDF in certain cases, and by refusing to intervene in others to prevent harm to the Palestinian residents'.[38]

Historically, Palestinian legal rights have been expressed not by the rulings of the Israeli High Court but in a number of landmark UN Security Council resolutions, in particular resolutions 242 and 338. These emphasise the 'inadmissibility of the acquisition of territory by war' and call for an Israeli withdrawal from the territories occupied in 1967. Such resolutions have kept Palestinian rights on the international agenda long after 'facts on the ground' have rendered these expressions of international law irrelevant in Israel's eyes. It is up to the international community to ensure that the ICJ advisory opinion does not follow the same fate as these resolutions, ignored by Israel and honoured in the breach by UN member states which do nothing in practice to ensure Israel's compliance.

Israeli non-compliance is all the more likely given that the US House of Representatives, by an overwhelming bipartisan majority, condemned the advisory opinion, while commending President Bush for 'his leadership in marshalling opposition to the misuse of the ICJ'.[39] Congressional dismissal echoed the House's earlier and equally overwhelming majority vote for the Bush letter of April 2004, which endorsed Israel's future annexation of the large settlement blocs. This vote, in the words of one commentator, represented 'not just another pro-Israel . . . resolution, but an effective renunciation of the post-World War II international system based upon the premise of the illegitimacy of the expansion of a country's territory by military force'.[40] Armed with the letter from President Bush and bolstered by US dismissal of the ICJ opinion, the likelihood is that Israel will take the new frontier represented by the route of the wall, rather than the internationally recognised Green Line, as its territorial starting point in the event of future negotiations. The long interim period before such negotiations occur will be employed in consolidating Israel's hold over those parts of the West Bank that constitute 'an inseparable part of the State of Israel in any future agreement', according to Sharon.

In the face of the realpolitik of such 'facts on the ground', a just resolution of the conflict must be 'on the basis of international legitimacy', especially UN Resolutions 242 and 338. The ICJ advisory opinion must remain the authoritative legal statement concerning the wall and Palestinian legal rights, rather than the rulings of the Israeli High Court. In particular, the internationally recognised Green Line must determine the parameters of a two-state solution, and not new realities on the ground such as settlements and the wall, built in violation of international law and continued in defiance of the ICJ advisory opinion and UN General Assembly Resolution ES-10/15.

UN experts mark anniversary of ICJ 'wall opinion' call on Israel to halt construction of the wall[41]

The eight undersigned Special Procedures mandate holders of the United Nations Commission on Human Rights issued this appeal shortly after the one-year anniversary of the International Court of Justice (ICJ) Advisory Opinion ('Wall opinion'), concerning the Legal Consequences of the Construction of a Wall in the Occupied Palestinian Territory:

The International Court of Justice (ICJ) in its 9 July 2004 advisory opinion held, *inter alia*, that the construction of a Wall in the Occupied Palestinian Territory is illegal. . . . In August 2004, in resolution ES-10/15 the General Assembly called upon Israel and other parties to comply with their legal obligations as mentioned in the Opinion. . . . However, neither the General Assembly nor the Security Council have considered the Opinion since.

In large measure it seems that the ICJ's Opinion has been ignored in favour of negotiations conducted in terms of the Road Map process. The exact nature of these negotiations is unclear but it seems that they are not premised on compliance with the Opinion of the ICJ. They seem to accept the continued presence of some settlements, which were found by the ICJ to be unlawful, and by necessary implication the continued existence of some parts of the wall in Palestinian territory. In short, there seems to be an incompatibility between the Road Map negotiations and the Court's Opinion that should be of concern to the United Nations which is also a party to the Quartet. The United Nations clearly cannot make itself a party to negotiations that are not based on the Opinion of its own judicial body.

On this, the first-year anniversary of the ICJ Wall Opinion, the Special Rapporteurs would like to:

- affirm that the continued construction of the wall constitutes a violation of Israel's human rights obligations;
- call upon Israel to stop construction of the wall being built in the Occupied Palestinian Territory, including in and around East Jerusalem, to dismantle the structure therein situated, and to repeal or render ineffective all legislative and regulatory acts relating thereto;
- call upon Israel to make reparation for all damage caused by the construction of the wall;
- remind States that they are under an obligation not to recognize the illegal situation resulting from the construction of the wall and not to render aid or assistance in maintaining the situation created by such construction;
- draw attention to the fact that every effort should be made to ensure that the United Nations, operating within the Quartet and engaged in the Road Map process, does its utmost to ensure compliance with the ICJ Opinion and fulfils its role in upholding international human rights standards;
- call on the United Nations Commission on Human Rights to act on this matter.

Signed:

Special Rapporteur on the situation of human rights in the Palestinian territories occupied since 1967, Prof. John Dugard.

Special Rapporteur on adequate housing as a component of the right to an adequate standard of living, Mr Miloon Kothari.

Special Rapporteur on violence against women, its causes and consequences, Ms Yakin Erturk.

Special Rapporteur on the right to education, Mr Vernor Munoz Villalobos.

Special Rapporteur on the right of everyone to the enjoyment of the highest attainable standard of physical and mental health, Mr Paul Hunt.

Special Rapporteur on contemporary forms of racism, racial discrimination, xenophobia and related intolerance, Mr Doudou Diène.

Chairperson, Rapporteur, Working Group on arbitrary detention, Ms Leila Zerrougui.

Special Rapporteur on trafficking in persons, especially in women and children, Ms Sigma Huda.

NOTES

1. In addition to Gush Shalom, activist groups included the Israeli Campaign against House Demolitions <http://www.icahd.org/eng/>; Checkpoint Watch <http://www.machsom.watch.org/>; Taa'yush <http://www.taayush.org/>; Physicians for Human Rights <http://www.phr.org.il/phr/>; and Rabbis for Human Rights. <http://www.rhr.israel.net/> (all accessed on 18 October 2005).

2. Kobi Snitz, 'On recent Palestinian popular resistance and its Israeli support', <http://www.fdca.it/wall/media/anarwall_EN.pdf > (accessed on 18 October 2005). 'Although the form of organization is anarchist in the sense of [having] no centralized power and direct participatory democracy, most participants probably do not consider themselves anarchists.'

3. Gush Shalom, 'The wall must fall, must fall, must fall!', 13 December 2003. <http://www.palestinemonitor.org/eyewitness/Westbank/the_wall_must_fall.html> (accessed on 21 October 2005).

4. Lily Galili, 'Fence and defense', Ha'aretz, 21 March 2004.

5. 'Many Israelis worked with the International Solidarity Movement, but

there was a feeling of the need to make the fact [sic] that Israelis were resisting (with the same methods as the ISM). This was important both for the Israeli public and for the Palestinian public (and also internationally). Israelis also come from a different perspective and culture from the internationals and it's important to create an autonomist group resisting together with Palestinians and internationals, but as a separate group.' Uri Ayalon, 'Resisting the apartheid wall', <http://www.fdca.it/wall/media/anarwall_EN.pdf> (accessed on 18 October 2005).

6. As an indication of the confusion in many Palestinians' minds between Jews and Israelis, '[a]n Israeli demonstrator relates that she heard a Palestinian say proudly that "the Israelis" – meaning the demonstrators – had protected them from "the Jews", meaning the soldiers.' Meron Rappaport, 'Gandhi redux', *Ha'aretz*, 10 June 2005.

7. Ayed Morrar, 'The peaceful fall of Israel's wall', *The Electronic Intifada*, 15 July 2004.

8. 'The military court at Ofer Camp released Ayed within a few days, stating: "It is out of the question for the military commander to use his authority to order a person's administrative detention (arrest without trial) only because of his activity against the fence. This is a mistaken decision that does not stem from security considerations." A month later, the military court at the Ketziot detention camp released [his brother] Naim, stating that the military prosecution and the Shin Bet had misled the court by claiming he had been involved in terrorist activity and adding that protest activity against the fence does not constitute a cause for arrest.' Aviv Lavie, 'Picking their battles', *Ha'aretz*, 15 April 2004.

9. 'Hassan Yusuf [leader of Hamas in the West Bank] is not eager to adopt nonviolent struggle as the only path. "We have tried everything, and we will try this way too," he says. "If the occupation leaves peacefully, we are in favour of measures of peace, but it does not seem that this is what the occupation wants."' Rappaport, 'Gandhi redux'.

10. Uri Avnery, 'Justice, gas and tears', 3 July 2004, <http://www.redress.btinternet.co.uk/uavnery91.htm> (accessed on 18 October 2005).

11. Cynthia Johnston, 'Westerners brave tear gas in Israel barrier battle', Reuters, 24 May 2004.

12. According to Human Rights Watch, Israeli security forces killed more than 1,600 Palestinian civilians not involved in hostilities, including at least 500 children, between 29 September 2000 and 30 November 2004. As of May 2005, the IDF had initiated only 108 investigations into these

killings, resulting in 19 indictments and six convictions, the longest sentence being 20 months. Press Release, 'Israel: failure to probe civilian casualties fuels impunity', 22 June 2005. See also the Human Rights Watch report, *Promoting Impunity: the Israeli Military's Failure to Investigate Wrongdoing*, June 2005.

13. '[L]ast month, during a protest against the fence, this correspondent witnessed security forces firing tear gas and stun grenades into a peaceful demonstration. The firing continued for about 45 minutes before Palestinian youths began throwing stones.' Ben Lynfield, 'West Bank town tries to protest the wall non-violently', *Christian Science Monitor*, 6 May 2004.

14. 'Muhammad Hatib, one of the village chiefs, noticed a man who, with his face covered, started to throw stones at the soldiers. He ran towards him, shouting: "We decided not to throw stones! If you want to throw stones, do it in your own village, not ours! What village do you come from anyway?" The man turned towards him and attacked him, at the same time calling out to his associates, tearing the handkerchief from his face and donning a police cap. Thus the secret came out and was also documented by the camera: "Arabized" undercover soldiers had been sent into action. They started throwing stones at the security people in order to provide them with a pretext to attack us. The moment they were uncovered, they turned on the demonstrators nearest to them, drew revolvers and started to arrest them.' Uri Avnery, 'A tale of two demonstrations', 30 April 2005. <http://usa.mediamonitors.net/layout/set/print/content/view/full/14551> (accessed on 21 October 2005).

15. Jonathan Lis, 'Border police "lie about violence at fence protests"', *Ha'aretz*, 28 July 2005. 'In recent weeks, three judges harshly criticised troops after watching videotapes that nullified their allegations.'

16. An all-women's demonstration against the wall in Biddu in April 2004 was broken up by tear gas, stun grenades and mounted police, and Molly Malekar, director of the Bat Shalom Israeli feminist peace group was clubbed on the head by a mounted policewoman. Police claimed the women 'were engaged in a riot'. In another demonstration in the same village, Rabbi Arik Ascherman, executive director of Rabbis for Human Rights, tried to intervene on behalf of the boy being used as a human shield, and was himself handcuffed and forced to serve as a human shield. 'The local police commander, Shahar Yitzhaki, seized Ascherman by the throat and headbutted him, [a] rabbi said'. Lynfield, 'West Bank town tries to protest the wall non-violently.'

17. Roane Carey and Adam Shatz, 'Israel Plays With Fire', *The Nation*, 12 April 2004.

   Ironically, it was in Qibya, a village beside Budrus, that a young Ariel Sharon first came to prominence in 1953, when he led a reprisal raid for the killing of an Israeli woman and her two children. Sharon's commandos blew up 54 houses, killing 69 Palestinians, including women and children. 'In Budrus, they're convinced that Prime Minister Sharon is continuing what Captain Sharon began: In Qibya, he tried it with dynamite, now he's trying it with a fence.' Gideon Levy, 'The peaceful way works best', *Ha'aretz*, 11 February 2004.

18. See <www.stopthewall.org> (accessed on 18 October 2005).

19. The exception to official Palestinian inactivity was the Palestinian Negotiation Affairs Department but this, strictly speaking, is a PLO rather than a Palestinian Authority body. See <http://www.nad-plo.org> (accessed on 21 October 2005).

20. Although the head of the Palestinian Authority committee set up to investigate the charges stated that 'compelling evidence and documents adequate for indicting those involved were referred to the public prosecutor' in June 2004, no prosecution has resulted to date. Hasan Abu Nimah and Ali Abunimah, 'Deep-rooted corruption in Palestine', *The Electronic Intifada*, 23 June 2004.

21. Palestinian Legislative Council member Abdel Jawad Saleh, quoted in Nancy Updike, 'Hitting the wall', *LA Weekly*, 12–18 March 2004.

22. 'World Council of Churches calls for divestment from Israel', *Ha'aretz*, 24 February 2005. In the Boston suburb of Somerville, the Somerville Divestment Project is similarly attempting to persuade the Somerville Board of Aldermen to divest from Israeli bonds and from companies that profit from the Israeli occupation. See <http://www.divestmentproject. org> (accessed on 21 October 2005).

23. 'UN registry of damage to Palestinians from Israeli barrier moves step closer', *UN News*, 11 January 2005.

24. *Report of the Special Rapporteur of the Commission on Human Rights, John Dugard, on the situation of human rights in the Palestinian territories occupied by Israel since 1967: Israeli Practices Affecting the Human Rights of the Palestinian People in the Occupied Palestinian Territory, including East Jerusalem*, 18 August 2005, para 53.

25. Pat O'Connor, 'Israel is failing the moral test', *Ha'aretz*, 14 February 2004.

26. *Report of the Special Rapporteur of the Commission on Human Rights,*

John Dugard, on the situation of human rights in the Palestinian territories occupied by Israel since 1967: Israeli Practices Affecting the Human Rights of the Palestinian People in the Occupied Palestinian Territory, including East Jerusalem, 18 August 2005, Para. 163.

27. Amira Hass, 'Donor countries won't fund Israeli-planned separate roads for Palestinians', *Ha'aretz*, 30 November 2004.

28. Palestinian National Authority, *The Annexation and Expansion Wall: Impacts and Mitigation Measures*, May 2004. Local Aid Coordination Committee, *Wall Mitigation: Implications for Donors and Implementing Agencies Operating in Areas Affected by the Separation Barrier*, 30 January 2005.

29. International Court of Justice, *Advisory Opinion*, Para 151.

30. Peter Lagerquist, 'Fencing the last sky: Israel's "separation wall"', *Journal of Palestine Studies*, Volume 33, Number 2, Winter 2004, p. 27.

31. International Court of Justice, *Advisory Opinion*, Para, Para. 122.

32. Ibid., Para. 155

33. United Nations Security Council, 'Press statement on Israeli disengagement by Security Council President', 24 August 2005.

34. Ian Williams, 'Israeli wall on trial: venue shifts to the International Court of Justice', *Foreign Policy In Focus Commentary*, 10 February 2004.

35. *Israeli Practices Affecting the Human Rights of the Palestinian People in the Occupied Palestinian Territory, including East Jerusalem*, para. 55.

36. Ibid., Para. 50.

37. Speech delivered in Ramallah on first anniversary of ICJ advisory opinion. <http://www.palestine-pmc.com/details.asp?cat=4&id=2030> (accessed on 18 October 2005).

38. B'Tselem, *Land Grab*, p.133.

39. 'The congressional resolution also warned other countries not to utilize international humanitarian law with regard to the occupied West Bank, stating that nations would "risk a strongly negative impact on their relationship with the people and the government of the United States should they use the ICJ's advisory judgement as an excuse to interfere" with the US-managed peace process.' Stephen Zunes, 'Israeli human rights abuses and the US Attack on the United Nations and the NGO community', *Foreign Policy In Focus Policy Report*, 30 June 2005.

40. Stephen Zunes, 'Congress overwhelmingly endorses Ariel Sharon's annexation plans', *Foreign Policy In Focus Commentary*, 25 June 2004.

41. Statement issued 4 August 2005 to coincide with the first anniversary of the ICJ advisory opinion. Available at <http://www.unhchr.ch/huricane/huricane.nsf/0/8FD9E0FA6FBB46CBC1257053003086C9?opendocument> (accessed on 18 October 2005).

Index